Victoria

SWEET BAKING

SWEET
BAKING

HEARST BOOKS

NEW YORK

LIBRARY OF CONGRESS CATALOGING-IN-PUBLICATION

Victoria sweet baking / [editor, Miriam Rubin]. -- 1st ed.

    p.   cm.

Includes index.

ISBN 0-688-14469-1

1. Baking.   I. Rubin, Miriam.

TX763.V49   1997   97-5205

641.8'15--dc21   CIP0

PRINTED IN SINGAPORE

For Victoria

Nancy Lindemeyer, *Editor-in-Chief*

Susan Maher, *Art Director*

John Mack Carter, President, *Hearst Magazine Enterprises*

FIRST EDITION

1 2 3 4 5 6 7 8 9 10

EDITOR: DEBORAH MINTCHEFF

PROJECT EDITOR: MIRIAM RUBIN

DESIGNER: PATTI RATCHFORD

PRODUCED BY SMALLWOOD & STEWART, INC., NEW YORK CITY

CONTENTS

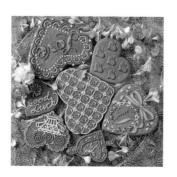

FOREWORD

Our moms usually start us out baking. Little fingers intently push cookie dough from the edge of a spoon under watchful eyes. When big people pies are getting made, youngsters have their own bits of pastry crust to sprinkle with sugar and cinnamon, so that they can have the thrill of watching them come out of the oven perfuming the kitchen with a scent never to be forgotten.

Perhaps this is why so many of us love to bake. And for people who don't bake often, holidays provide the opportunity for rituals, for baking to delight our friends and grace our holiday meals. We have encountered remarkable bakers during the years *Victoria* has been collecting recipes. Imagination and creativity seem to be almost as commonplace as flour and sugar.

Whether you learned to bake as a child or took up this delicious pastime later on, you'll find on these pages recipes to add to your cherished list. There is some serious baking here to put your skills to the test and to satisfy your appetite for producing fabulous desserts. Included, too, are simple recipes whose charm never wavers. Bakers may never have found such a treasure before.

Enjoy *Sweet Baking*. How delighted I will be to discover that you have made many of these recipes part of your family tradition, perhaps adding your own touches of inspiration along the way.

Nancy Lindemeyer

Editor in Chief, *Victoria* Magazine

Sour Cherry Pie

(recipe on page 25)

FRUIT

Fruit desserts take us straight back to our childhood ~ in winter, memories of cozy and comfortable kitchens filled with the heady aromas of stewing apples and ripe juicy plums steeped in nutmeg and cinnamon; in summer, visions of sun-filled afternoons spent gathering and preparing the bounty of the season for what were surely the world's best pies and tarts. The recipes in this chapter are all the traditional ones of our nostalgia and more, magically balancing the sweetness and tartness of fruits fairly bursting with flavor. Freshly picked summer peaches take a star turn in a layer cake brimming with whipped cream; crisp tart baking apples and dark rum transform a simple pie into a sublime creation; syrup-infused double lemon cake indulges our senses. These are the desserts we know will make us happy, rich with the tastes we love.

APPLE RUM PIE

Makes 6 servings

The pastry for this pie is quite delicate. Chill it thoroughly before rolling it out and it will be easier to handle. If the day is warm, roll the dough out on a baking sheet and place in the freezer until firm.

FLAKY PASTRY

1¾ cups all-purpose flour

3 tablespoons sugar

⅛ teaspoon salt

6 tablespoons cold unsalted butter, cut into bits

⅓ cup solid white vegetable shortening

APPLE RUM FILLING

½ cup sugar

1 tablespoon all-purpose flour

2 teaspoons ground cinnamon

½ teaspoon ground nutmeg

2 pounds Granny Smith apples, peeled, cored and cut into ½-inch thick slices (7 cups)

⅓ cup heavy cream

¼ cup dark rum

1 large egg beaten with ¼ cup cold water

1. To make the flaky pastry, put the flour, sugar, and salt into a food processor and pulse to mix. Add the butter and the shortening and pulse several times, until the mixture forms a coarse meal.

2. With the processor running, add 3 to 4 tablespoons of ice water and pulse until the dough pulls away from the side of the bowl and forms a ball.

3. Divide the dough into two-third and one-third portions. Shape each into a disk, wrap in plastic, and refrigerate for 1 hour, or until firm.

4. To make the apple rum filling, in a large bowl, stir together the sugar, flour, cinnamon, and nutmeg. Add the apples and toss to mix well. Add the cream and rum and mix again.

5. Preheat the oven to 450°F. Set out a 9-inch removable bottom tart pan.

A formal fluting of pastry surrounds a generous filling of apples.

6. Roll the larger piece of dough on a heavily floured surface into a 12-inch round. Line the tart pan with the dough. (The dough will be sticky and quite fragile to handle.) Roll the smaller piece of dough into a 9½-inch round.

7. Spoon the apple filling into the pastry shell and place the smaller pastry round over the filling. Trim, seal, and flute the edges. Cut any pastry scraps into decorative shapes and arrange on top. Cut slits in the top crust to allow steam to escape and brush the pie with a thin even layer of the beaten egg.

8. Bake for 20 minutes. Reduce the oven temperature to 375°F and bake for 40 minutes longer, or until the filling is bubbling in the center and the apples are tender. If necessary, tent the pie with foil towards the end of the baking time to prevent the crust from over-browning. Cool the pie on a rack.

TARTE DES DEMOISELLES TATIN

Makes 8 to 10 servings

Tarte Tatin, an upside-down apple tart, is a classic dessert in France. It was made famous in the late nineteenth century by the two Tatin sisters who served it in their hotel in the Loire region of France. It's treasured for the deep mahogany color and the intense flavor the apples develop as they slowly caramelize in butter and sugar. Pears, or a combination of apples and pears, make a delicious tart as well.

PASTRY

1½ cups all-purpose flour

½ cup confectioners' sugar

Pinch of salt

½ cup (1 stick) cold unsalted butter, cut into bits

2 large egg yolks

1 tablespoon brandy

Grated zest of 1 medium-size lemon

APPLE FILLING

¾ cup confectioners' sugar

4 pounds small Golden Delicious apples, peeled, cored and cut into eighths
(12 to 15 small apples)

6 tablespoons unsalted butter, melted

Ground cinnamon (optional)

Crème fraîche, for serving
(see box page 16)

1. To make the pastry, in a large bowl, stir together the flour, confectioners' sugar, and the salt. With a pastry blender or two knives, cut in the butter until the mixture forms a coarse meal.

2. With a fork, beat in the egg yolks, brandy, and lemon zest until a dough forms. Gather the dough into a smooth ball. Wrap it in plastic and refrigerate for at least 30 minutes, or until it is firm.

3. To make the apple filling, use a heavy 10-inch oven-proof skillet with straight sides, at least 2 inches high. Sprinkle the bottom of the skillet with 6 tablespoons of the confectioners' sugar.

This legendary upside down apple tart is spectacular.

4. Arrange a layer of apple wedges, rounded side down, in tight concentric circles over the sugar. Brush the apples with some of the butter, and if desired, dust with a little cinnamon. Repeat the layers until you have used all the apples.

5. Cover the skillet tightly with a lid or buttered foil. Cook over medium-low to low heat for 1 hour, gently shaking the pan occasionally, or until the apples are tender and the sugar begins to caramelize. Be careful not to burn the sugar. Remove the skillet from the heat. (If the apples become tender before the sugar caramelizes, remove the cover and gently simmer the apples to evaporate the juices and caramelize the sugar.)

6. Preheat the oven to 400°F.

7. Roll the pastry on a lightly floured surface into a round slightly larger than the top of the skillet. Place the pastry over the apples and trim it even with the inside edge of the skillet, so that the pastry rests directly on the filling.

8. Bake for 15 to 20 minutes, until the pastry is flaky and golden brown. Let the tart cool in the pan on a rack for 5 minutes.

9. Invert the tart onto a high-sided serving plate to catch the juices. Carefully remove any apples that have adhered to the skillet and rearrange them atop the tart. Serve the tart accompanied by a bowl of crème fraîche.

Crème Fraîche

The French serve crème fraîche with sweet and savory food alike. This American version has a slightly nutty tangy flavor, the thickness of good-quality sour cream, and a silky smooth texture.

Combine 1 cup heavy cream with ½ cup sour cream in a glass bowl. Cover and let stand in a warm, draft-free place for 12 hours or overnight, until thickened. Refrigerate for another 24 hours, or until very thick. Crème fraîche can be stored in the refrigerator for up to 1 week. Makes 1½ cups.

APRICOT PRUNE TARTLETS

Makes 8 tartlets

These petit tarts, easily prepared from ingredients you probably have on hand, are perfect for unexpected guests. Try to find tart California dried apricots for these pastries; they have more bite than the sweeter Turkish variety.

12 to 16 dried apricot halves

12 to 16 pitted prunes

1 cup boiling water

One 17¼-ounce package frozen puff pastry (2 sheets), thawed according to package directions

¼ cup sugar

1. Preheat the oven to 400°F. Set out two baking sheets.

2. Place the apricots and prunes in separate small bowls. Pour half the boiling water into each bowl and let the fruit stand for 5 minutes, or until softened; drain.

3. Unfold one sheet of puff pastry on a lightly floured surface. Press together the seams to seal. Using a floured 4-inch biscuit cutter, cut the pastry into 4 rounds, saving the scraps for another use. Repeat with the remaining pastry sheet.

4. Arrange the pastry rounds on the baking sheets. Top each round with 3 or 4 pieces of each fruit and sprinkle them with the sugar.

5. Bake the tartlets for 15 minutes, or until the pastry is puffed and golden and the fruit is glazed. Serve the tartlets warm.

ORANGE WHIPPED CREAM CAKE

Makes 8 servings

Chiffon cake, developed in the 1920's, is a variation on angel food cake. It was a novelty in its day because it was prepared with oil instead of a solid shortening such as butter. The addition of oil keeps the cake moist and the crumb light. Since the cake batter needs to cling to the sides of the pan as it rises in the oven, butter isn't called for to grease the pan, either.

ORANGE CHIFFON CAKE

1 cup plus 2 tablespoons sifted cake flour

¾ cup granulated sugar

1½ teaspoons baking powder

½ teaspoon salt

¼ cup canola or vegetable oil

4 large eggs, separated (2 of the yolks are for the filling)

¼ cup plus 2 tablespoons freshly squeezed orange juice

¼ teaspoon cream of tartar

ORANGE CURD FILLING

1 cup granulated sugar

2 tablespoons cornstarch

½ teaspoon salt

1 cup freshly squeezed orange juice

2 tablespoons grated orange zest

2 tablespoons freshly squeezed lemon juice

2 tablespoons unsalted butter

CREAM FROSTING

2 cups heavy cream

1 teaspoon vanilla extract

2 tablespoons confectioners' sugar

2 tablespoons buttermilk

1 cup sliced seedless green grapes

Fresh grape leaves, for garnish (optional)

1. Preheat the oven to 325°F. Set out two 7½-inch springform pans. (Do not use nonstick pans.)
2. To make the orange chiffon cake, sift the cake flour, granulated sugar, baking powder, and salt into the medium-size bowl of an electric mixer.

Tangy cream cheese frosting anchors light-as-air chiffon layers.

3. Make a well in the center of the flour mixture. Add the oil, 2 of the egg yolks, and the orange juice, in that order. Beat at high speed for 1 minute, or until satin smooth. Wash the beaters.

4. In the large bowl of the mixer, at high speed, beat the egg whites and cream of tartar until stiff peaks form when the beaters are lifted. With a large rubber spatula, fold the orange-juice batter into the beaten whites. Pour the batter evenly into the prepared pans and gently smooth the tops.

5. Bake for 40 minutes, or until a toothpick inserted in the center comes out clean and the center springs back when lightly touched. Invert and completely cool the cakes upside down by resting each on the rims of three empty pans.

6. Run a thin metal spatula around the edges to loosen the cakes and remove the pan sides. Gently lift the cakes from the pan bottoms with the spatula. With a long serrated knife, slice each cake in half horizontally.

7. While the cakes are baking, make the orange curd filling. In a small heavy saucepan, stir together the granulated sugar, cornstarch, and salt.

8. Stir in the orange juice and the remaining 2 egg yolks. Cook over medium-high heat, whisking constantly, until the mixture thickens and boils. Remove from the heat, add the orange zest, lemon juice, and butter, and stir until the butter is melted.

9. Pour the filling into a medium-size bowl. Press plastic wrap directly onto the surface of the filling and refrigerate until it is just cooled.

10. To make the cream frosting, in the chilled small bowl of the mixer, at high speed, beat the cream and vanilla until soft peaks form. Gradually add the confectioners' sugar, beating until stiff. Stir in the buttermilk.

11. Fold 1 cup of the frosting into the filling; cover and refrigerate the remaining frosting while you are filling the cake.

12. Place one cake layer on a serving plate. Spread evenly with some of the orange filling and arrange all the grapes on top. Add the second and third cake layers, spreading each with orange filling. Top with the last cake layer.

13. Frost the cake top and sides with the cream frosting and refrigerate until ready to serve. Garnish with grape leaves, if desired. Refrigerate any leftovers.

ORANGE POPPY SEED CAKE

Makes 8 servings

⅔ cup milk

2 tablespoons grated orange zest

¼ cup poppy seeds

1 tablespoon vanilla extract

1½ cups all-purpose flour

1½ teaspoons baking powder

½ cup (1 stick) unsalted butter, at room temperature

¾ cup sugar

4 large egg whites, at room temperature

1. In a small saucepan, over moderately-low heat, bring the milk and orange zest just to boiling. Remove from the heat and allow to cool to room temperature. Stir in the poppy seeds and vanilla.

2. Preheat the oven to 350°F. Generously butter a 1-quart decorative tube mold. Dust the mold with flour, shaking out the excess.

3. Sift together the flour and baking powder.

4. In the large bowl of an electric mixer, at high speed, beat the butter until it is light and fluffy. Add ½ cup plus 2 tablespoons of the sugar, a little at a time, beating until it is well blended.

5. Reduce the mixer speed to low and add the flour mixture in three additions, alternately with the orange-scented milk, beating until just mixed after each addition, beginning and ending with the flour mixture.

6. Wash the beaters. In the medium-size bowl of the mixer, at high speed, beat the egg whites until soft peaks form. Gradually add the remaining 2 tablespoons of sugar and beat until stiff peaks form when the beaters are lifted.

7. Whisk one-third of the whites into the batter. With a rubber spatula, fold in the remaining whites gently but thoroughly. Pour into the prepared mold.

8. Bake for 45 minutes, or until the cake is golden. Cool in the pan on a rack for 10 minutes. Run a thin metal spatula around the edge to loosen the cake and turn the cake out onto the rack to cool completely.

BLUEBERRY AND PECAN CRUNCH PIE

Makes 10 to 12 servings

This sumptuous pie doesn't need any adornment, but a small scoop of butter pecan ice cream would be just right. Wait until blueberries are sweet and fat before you even think about making this pie. You can dress it up with a ruffle of whipped cream for a dinner party, or forgo the cream, tuck it into vintage wicker pie basket, and bring it along on an elegant late summer picnic in the park.

1 recipe Charlotte's Pie Crust (page 198)

½ cup pound cake crumbs (page 86)

Grated zest and juice of 1 medium-size orange

Grated zest and juice of 1 medium-size lemon

BLUEBERRY FILLING

1 cup sugar

3 tablespoons cornstarch

1 tablespoon ground cinnamon

½ teaspoon peeled and grated fresh ginger

¼ teaspoon ground nutmeg

3 pints blueberries (about 8 cups)

PECAN CRUNCH TOPPING

1 cup chopped pecans

1 cup all-purpose flour

¾ cup sugar

1 tablespoon ground cinnamon

1 cup (2 sticks) cold unsalted butter, cut into bits

Whipped cream, for garnish

1. Preheat the oven to 375°F. Set out a 9½-inch springform pan.

2. Roll the pie crust on a lightly floured work surface into a 16-inch round. Line the bottom and side of the springform pan with the pastry. Trim the pastry just slightly higher than the top edge of the pan, then turn it under and press it against the top edge. Sprinkle the pound cake crumbs over the bottom.

3. To prepare the blueberry filling, in a small bowl, stir together the sugar, cornstarch, cinnamon, ginger, and nutmeg until they are well blended.

4. In a large bowl, gently mix the blueberries and the zest and juice from the orange and lemon. With a rubber spatula, fold the sugar mixture into the blueberries and pour the filling into the pastry shell. Place the pan on a baking sheet.

5. Bake for 15 minutes.

6. While pie is baking, make the crunch topping. In a large bowl, stir together the pecans, flour, sugar, and cinnamon. With a pastry blender or two knives, cut in the butter until the mixture forms coarse crumbs.

7. Sprinkle the crunch topping evenly over the partially baked pie. Reduce the oven temperature to 350°F and bake for 60 minutes longer, or until the berries are juicy and tender and the pastry is lightly browned and crisp. If the topping begins to overbrown during baking, tent the pie loosely with foil.

8. Let the pie cool completely in the pan on a rack. (The filling will settle during cooling.) Loosen and remove the pan sides.

9. Just before serving, pipe a high ruffle of whipped cream around the top edge of the pie. Refrigerate any leftovers.

Fresh Blueberries

Blueberries are available nearly eight months of the year, but their peak season is from mid-June to mid-August. Store blueberries in the refrigerator, covered, and rinse just before you use them, discarding any wrinkled or moldy berries.

Out of season, use the frozen variety, but do not rinse them or they'll clump together. Also, don't thaw blueberries unless a recipe indicates that you should.

To freeze blueberries, choose firm, ripe berries and do not rinse them. Either put the berry basket in a freezer bag, or put the berries in a jelly-roll pan in a single layer and freeze them. Pack the frozen berries in freezer bags or containers and return them to the freezer. For convenience, freeze measured amounts of berries (1 cup is handy), and be sure to label and date the bags.

BLUEBERRY CRISP

Makes 6 servings

Crisps are little more than sweetened fresh fruit with a crunchy topping of flour, sugar, and butter. They are wonderfully homey and welcoming ~ just right for an impromptu dessert get together. Crisps are most often accompanied by softly whipped cream or slightly softened ice cream ~ fresh peach or raspberry ice cream would be sublime. Here, the fresh blueberries are combined with the more unusual dried blueberries and a little port, resulting in a crisp with an intense blueberry flavor that is fragrant and intoxicatingly rich.

BLUEBERRY FILLING

⅓ cup dried blueberries

⅓ cup port wine

6 cups fresh blueberries

CRUMB TOPPING

¾ cup packed light or dark brown sugar

¾ cup all-purpose flour

1 teaspoon ground nutmeg

½ cup (1 stick) cold unsalted butter, cut into bits

1. To make the blueberry filling, in a medium-size bowl, stir together the dried blueberries and port wine and let them stand for 30 minutes.
2. Preheat the oven to 375°F. Butter six 12-ounce custard cups or six individual baking dishes. Place the baking dishes on a baking sheet.
3. Add the fresh blueberries to the dried blueberries and mix gently. Spoon 1 cup of the berry mixture into each prepared baking dish.
4. To make the crumb topping, in a medium-size bowl, stir together the brown sugar, flour, and nutmeg until well blended. With a pastry blender, cut in the butter until the mixture forms a fine meal. Sprinkle over the berries.
5. Bake for 20 to 25 minutes, until the fruit is bubbling and the topping is crisp and golden brown. Serve the crisps warm.

SOUR CHERRY PIE

(PHOTOGRAPH ON PAGE 10)

Makes 8 to 10 servings

It's a labor of love to pit cherries, requiring a comfortable porch rocker, clothes that can be stained with cherry juices, and a long, warm, summer's day. A cherry pitter is a handy tool, but if you don't have one, an opened-up paper clip works just as well. Simply insert one end into a cherry, let it catch on the pit, and pull it out.

1 recipe Charlotte's Pie Crust
   (page 198)

CHERRY FILLING

5 cups fresh sour cherries

1 tablespoon freshly squeezed
   lemon juice

1 teaspoon cherry brandy

½ teaspoon almond extract

1 cup sugar, plus additional
   sugar for the crust

¼ cup cornstarch

1 tablespoon unsalted butter

1 tablespoon half-and-half

1. Roll two-thirds of the pastry on a very heavily floured surface into a 12-inch round. Fit the pastry into a 10-inch pie plate and refrigerate. Roll the remaining pastry into an 11-inch round and cut it into ¾-inch wide strips. Place the strips on a baking sheet, cover, and refrigerate. Preheat the oven to 400°F.

2. To make the cherry filling, in a large bowl, toss the cherries with the lemon juice, cherry brandy, and almond extract. In a small bowl, stir the sugar and cornstarch until blended. Pour the sugar mixture over the cherries and toss to mix well.

3. Spoon the cherry filling into the pastry shell and dot with the butter. Crisscross the pastry strips in a lattice pattern over the top of the pie, pressing the strips to the edge of the pastry. Fold the pastry edge over and crimp to seal. Brush with half-and-half and sprinkle with sugar. Place the pie plate on a baking sheet.

4. Bake for 20 minutes. Reduce the oven temperature to 350°F and bake for 45 to 60 minutes longer, until the pastry is nicely browned and the filling is bubbling near the center. Transfer to a rack to cool. Serve warm or at room temperature.

PEACH ALMOND TART

Makes 6 to 8 servings

For this tart, seek out locally grown peaches that have been ripened on the tree; the fruit will be lush and full of flavor. Look for signs of ripeness ~ a creamy or gold undercoloring on the skin and a sweet fragrance. If the peaches need to be ripened further, let them stand for a day or two at room temperature, and once they yield to gentle pressure, store them in the refrigerator.

ALMOND PASTRY

1¼ cups all-purpose flour

½ cup ground almonds

2 tablespoons confectioners' sugar

¼ teaspoon salt

6 tablespoons cold unsalted butter, cut into bits

1 large egg yolk, beaten with 3 tablespoons ice water

PEACH FILLING

4 cups sliced peeled peaches (about 5)

2 tablespoons freshly squeezed orange juice

½ teaspoon almond extract

1 tablespoon cornstarch

4 tablespoons granulated sugar

¼ cup sliced almonds

2 tablespoons cold unsalted butter, cut into bits

1. To make the almond pastry, in a large bowl, stir together the flour, ground almonds, confectioners' sugar, and salt. With a pastry blender or two knives, cut in the butter until the mixture forms a coarse meal.

2. Add the beaten yolk to the flour mixture and mix with a fork until the flour is moistened. Gather the dough into a ball, shape it into a disk, wrap in plastic, and refrigerate for at least 30 minutes, or until firm.

3. Roll the dough on a lightly floured surface into a 12-inch round. Fit the pastry into a 10-inch tart pan and trim the edges. Cover and refrigerate for 1 hour.

4. Preheat the oven to 425°F. Line the pastry with a double thickness of foil and fill the foil with dried beans or pie weights. Place the tart pan on a baking sheet.

Nothing says summer more than an extravagant fresh peach pie.

5. Bake the pastry for 15 minutes. Remove the foil and beans and bake 3 to 5 minutes longer, until lightly browned. Transfer the pastry to a rack to cool completely.

6. Reduce the oven to 375°F.

7. To make the peach filling, in a large bowl, toss the peaches with the orange juice and almond extract. In a small bowl, stir together the cornstarch and 3 tablespoons of the sugar. Add this to the peaches and toss gently to blend.

8. Arrange the peach slices in concentric circles in the cooled tart shell. Drizzle the peaches with any juices left in the bowl. Top with the sliced almonds, sprinkle with the remaining 1 tablespoon sugar, and dot with the butter.

9. Bake for 45 to 50 minutes, until the peaches are tender and the juices bubbling. Transfer the tart to a rack to cool and serve it while it is still warm.

PEACHES AND CREAM CAKE

Makes 10 to 12 servings

This spectacular cake stands two glorious layers high and is generously filled and topped with freshly sugared peaches and whipped cream flavored with peach wine. This is strictly summer fare ~ winter peaches just are not succulent enough.

CAKE

2½ cups all-purpose flour

2¼ teaspoons baking powder

½ teaspoon salt

2 cups granulated sugar

4 large eggs, at room
   temperature

1 cup vegetable oil

1 cup peach wine

1 teaspoon vanilla extract

PEACHES AND CREAM
   TOPPING

3 tablespoons granulated sugar

4 cups thickly sliced peaches
   (about 5)

1½ cups heavy cream

¼ cup confectioners' sugar

2 tablespoons peach wine

1. Preheat the oven to 350°F. Generously butter two 9-inch layer-cake pans. Dust the pans with flour, shaking out the excess.

2. To make the cake, stir together the flour, baking powder, and salt.

3. In the large bowl of an electric mixer, at medium speed, beat the granulated sugar and the eggs for 30 seconds, scraping the side of the bowl often.

4. Add the oil, peach wine, vanilla, and the flour mixture. Reduce the mixer speed to low and beat until just blended. Increase the mixer to medium speed and beat the batter for 1 minute, or until it is smooth. (The batter will be thin.) Pour the batter into the prepared pans.

5. Bake for 35 minutes, or until the center springs back when the cake is lightly touched. (The cake will begin to pull away from the side of the pan before the center of the cake is done.)

Moist and delicious, this exciting cake calls for a large gathering.

6. Let the cakes cool in the pans on racks for 10 minutes. Run a metal spatula around the edges of the pans to loosen the cakes and turn them out onto the racks to cool completely.

7. While the cakes cool, make the peaches and cream topping. In a medium-size bowl, gently fold the granulated sugar into the peaches.

8. In the chilled medium-size bowl of the mixer, at high speed, beat the cream until soft peaks form. Gradually add the confectioners' sugar and peach wine, beating until stiff peaks form.

9. Place one cake on a serving plate. Spoon half of the cream topping over the cake, spreading it roughly with a spatula. Arrange half of the sugared peach slices in concentric circles over the cream.

10. Top with the second cake and spread the remaining cream over the top. Arrange the remaining peach slices over the cream and spoon any peach juices over the cream. Refrigerate any leftovers.

PEAR MERINGUE TART

Makes 6 servings

PASTRY

2 cups all-purpose flour

½ teaspoon salt

½ cup (1 stick) cold unsalted butter, cut into bits

3 tablespoons solid white vegetable shortening

PECAN MERINGUE

6 large egg whites, at room temperature

1 cup confectioners' sugar

1 teaspoon vanilla extract

1 cup pecans, finely ground

MAPLE POACHED PEARS

2 cups packed light or dark brown sugar

½ cup pure maple syrup

3 large firm-ripe pears, peeled, halved and cored

TOPPING

1 cup heavy cream

2 tablespoons granulated sugar

⅛ teaspoon ground cinnamon

2 tablespoons pear brandy

Chopped pecans, for garnish

1. To make the pastry, in a food processor, place the flour and salt and pulse to mix. Add the butter and shortening and pulse several times, until the mixture forms a coarse meal.

2. With the processor running, gradually add 4 to 5 tablespoons of ice water, and process until the dough pulls away from the side of the work bowl and forms a ball. Divide the dough in half, shape each half into a disk, wrap in plastic, and refrigerate for 30 minutes, or until chilled.

3. Preheat the oven to 400°F. Set out two heavy baking sheets.

4. Roll half of the dough on a floured surface into a rectangle slightly larger than 12 by 5 inches. Trim the edges. Transfer the pastry to one of the baking sheets and prick all over with a fork. Repeat with the second piece of dough.

5. Bake for 15 to 18 minutes, until nicely browned. Transfer the pastry layers to racks to cool completely. Reduce the oven temperature to 350°F.

6. To make the pecan meringue, in the large bowl of an electric mixer, at high

Pears nestle on clouds of meringue set atop a traditional galette.

speed, beat the egg whites until soft peaks form. Gradually add the confectioners' sugar and vanilla and beat until stiff peaks form when the beaters are lifted. Fold in the ground pecans.

7. Return the pastry layers to the baking sheets and spread them evenly with the meringue. Bake for 15 minutes, or until the meringue is lightly browned and set. Return the pastry layers to the racks to cool completely.

8. Meanwhile, make the maple-poached pears. In a large saucepan, stir together 4 cups of water, the brown sugar, and maple syrup. Bring the mixture to a boil over medium-high heat, stirring to dissolve the sugar.

9. Add the pears to the boiling syrup and reduce the heat to medium-low so that the syrup is at a gentle simmer. Cover and simmer for 5 to 15 minutes, until the pears are tender when pierced with a fork. Remove the pears from the syrup with a slotted spoon and let them drain and cool on paper towels.

10. Just before serving, make the topping and assemble the tarts. In the chilled small bowl of the mixer, at high speed, beat the cream, granulated sugar, and cinnamon until soft peaks form. Gradually add the brandy and beat until stiff.

11. Spread half of the cream over each meringue pastry layer. Top each pastry with three pear halves, flat side down, and garnish with chopped pecans.

12. To serve, cut each pastry into thirds with a serrated knife, cutting the pastry between the pear halves. Refrigerate any leftovers.

PASTRY GÂTEAUX
WITH RASPBERRY AND CREAM

Makes 6 servings

1 sheet frozen puff pastry
(from a 17¼-ounce
package), thawed according
to package directions

ORANGE SAUCE

1 cup freshly squeezed
orange juice

2 tablespoons granulated sugar

1 tablespoon cornstarch

2 tablespoons Grand Marnier

CREAM AND BERRY
FILLING

¾ cup heavy cream

2 tablespoons granulated sugar

6 tablespoons raspberry jam

2 cups fresh raspberries or
thinly sliced strawberries

2 tablespoons confectioners'
sugar

1. Preheat the oven to 375°F.

2. Gently unfold the pastry onto an unbuttered baking sheet. Cut it lengthwise into thirds, making three 10- by 3-inch strips. Prick the strips with a fork.

3. Bake for 25 to 30 minutes, until puffed and golden. Transfer the pastry strips to a rack to cool completely.

4. To make the orange sauce, in a small saucepan, over medium heat, bring the orange juice and granulated sugar to a boil, stirring to dissolve the sugar. Reduce the heat to low and simmer for 3 minutes.

5. In a cup, dissolve the cornstarch in 1 tablespoon of cold water and whisk into the orange juice. Increase the heat to medium-high and bring the sauce to a boil, stirring, until the mixture thickens. Remove from the heat and stir in the Grand Marnier. Place a sheet of plastic wrap directly onto the surface of the sauce and let the sauce cool.

6. To make the cream filling, in the chilled medium-size bowl of an electric mixer, at high speed, beat the cream and granulated sugar until stiff peaks form.

7. To assemble the cake, with a serrated knife, cut each pastry strip into three equal

Crunchy puff pastry contrasts with a creamy, fruit-studded filling.

pieces, trimming the edges even. Carefully divide each piece into two layers, removing any damp inner webbing. Reserve six attractive pieces for the tops.

8. Spread ½ tablespoon of the jam, and then 2 to 3 tablespoons of cream filling on each of the remaining twelve pastry pieces. Top each with a sprinkling of raspberries. Stack the filled layers, making six pastries, and top each with one of the reserved pastry pieces.

9. Sift the confectioners' sugar over the top of the pastries. Use a very hot metal skewer to create a caramelized crisscross pattern in the sugar, if desired.

10. Spoon some of the orange sauce in a pool on each of six dessert plates, top with a pastry, and serve immediately. Refrigerate any leftovers.

PLUM TART

Makes 8 servings

PASTRY

2 cups all-purpose flour

Pinch of salt

½ cup (1 stick) plus 1
   tablespoon unsalted butter,
   at room temperature

PLUM FILLING

10 purple or yellow plums
   (2 to 3 ounces each)

¼ cup sugar

1. To make the pastry, in a food processor, combine the flour and salt and pulse to mix. Add the butter and pulse several times, until blended.

2. With the processor running, add 2 tablespoons of cold water, 1 tablespoon at a time, processing until the dough forms a ball. Shape the dough into a disk, wrap in plastic, and let it stand at room temperature for 1 to 2 hours.

3. Meanwhile, make the plum filling. Quarter and pit 6 of the plums. In a heavy medium-size nonreactive saucepan, combine the quartered plums with ⅓ cup of water and the sugar. Bring to a boil over medium heat, stirring constantly. Reduce the heat to low, and simmer, uncovered, stirring often, for 25 minutes, or until the mixture is very thick. Remove from the heat and let stand until warm.

4. Preheat the oven to 425°F. Set out a 10-inch tart pan.

5. Quarter and pit the remaining plums.

6. Roll the dough on a lightly floured surface into a 12½-inch round. (The pastry is tender and will crack easily—press it back together with your fingers.) Fit the dough into the tart pan and trim the edge with the top of the pan.

7. Spread the cooked plums in the bottom of the pastry shell. Top with the uncooked plums, skin side down, evenly spaced. Place the tart on a baking sheet.

8. Bake for 45 minutes, or until the crust is nicely browned and the plum juices are bubbling near the center. Transfer the tart to a rack to cool.

A crisp pastry shell explodes with colorful, sweet plums.

Heavenly Flavor Marriages Lemon and ginger are a glamorous pair—the acidity and sweetness of lemon counterbalances the sharp, aromatic earthiness of ginger. There are other great flavor partnerships as well. The following classic and exotic combinations make any dessert special: Chocolate and Tangerine • Vanilla and Cream • Apples and Cinnamon • Pineapple and Honey • Coconut and Brown Sugar • Strawberries and Lime • Watermelon and Mint • Banana and Butterscotch.

Elizabeth On 37th

Designed by James Oglethorpe in 1733, the city of Savannah has retained much of its stately charm. Grand old mansions, all meticulously maintained, grace the city's beautiful squares, and the shady streets are elegantly lined with mature magnolias and pine trees.

Situated just south of Savannah's historic center, the house that is home to 'Elizabeth on 37th' is one of the South's purest examples of Southern architecture. So it is fitting that the restaurant's kitchen should pay homage to the culinary history of the South. A serious student of food, Elizabeth Terry is the ardent custodian of the fine old recipes of the eighteenth and nineteenth centuries, and one taste of her memorable desserts is more than enough to keep the old sweet song of Georgia on one's mind—her famous Peach and Blueberry Pie, for example. Guests flock to the restaurant year after year, when the Georgia

The charm of the South: elegant settings, fine desserts.

peach harvest ripens, especially for luscious slices. And there is her Pecan Almond Tart—bursting with local pecans—which retains the fresh, natural flavors of the Old South.

Mounds of raspberries bury the chocolatey-morsels in her delicious Chocolate Cake, and, although it is already moist beyond belief, her Chocolate, Cinnamon, and Apple Cake is richly drizzled with a chocolate cream frosting.

On a lighter note, her refreshing Mango Sorbet is scoped into a pedestal of airy meringue, and her Savannah Cream Cake, towering angel food with sherried custard, is sure to enchant even the most discerning dessert lover.

These are desserts to savor; surrounded by the restaurants lush garden oasis. With a balmy breeze and moonlight streaming through the trees, what, after all, could be more romantic than to linger over an elegant dessert such as Elizabeth's enticing version of crème brulée.

STRAWBERRY RHUBARB PIE

Makes 8 servings

⅔ cup sugar, plus additional sugar for sprinkling

2 tablespoons plus 1 teaspoon instant tapioca

½ teaspoon ground cinnamon

1¼ pounds rhubarb, cut into ½-inch slices (4 cups)

10 ounces small strawberries, halved (1½ cups)

1 recipe Old-Fashioned Dough (page 199)

1 large egg beaten with 3 tablespoons cold water

1. In a large bowl, whisk together the sugar, tapioca, and cinnamon. Add the rhubarb and strawberries; toss gently to mix. Let stand for 15 minutes.

2. Preheat the oven to 425°F. Set out a 9-inch pie plate.

3. Roll out two-thirds of the pastry on a lightly floured work surface into a 12-inch round. Fit the pastry into the pie plate.

4. For the lattice top, roll the remaining pastry into a 12- to 13-inch round. Cut into eight 1½-inch wide strips. Brush the dough strips with the beaten egg and sprinkle with sugar.

5. Spoon the rhubarb and strawberry filling into the pastry shell, mounding it in the center. Arrange the dough strips over the filling in a crisscross pattern.

6. Trim the crust edge and lattice strips to a 1-inch overhang. Fold the crust edge up over the lattice strips to form a thick edge, then flute the edge with your thumb and forefinger. Place the pie plate on a baking sheet.

7. Bake for 20 minutes. Reduce the oven temperature to 375°F and bake 40 to 45 minutes longer, until the pastry is well browned and the juices are bubbling. Transfer the pie to a rack to cool to room temperature.

STRAWBERRY SHORTCAKE

Makes 8 servings

As with many old-fashioned desserts, the all-American shortcake provokes debate, controversy, and fierce loyalty. Some bakers proclaim that authentic shortcake is made with biscuits ~ some say that sponge or angel food cake can also be used. Many bakers crush their berries, while others prefer them sliced or quartered. One thing that everyone agrees upon is that the whipped cream must be real ~ whether it is sweetened or not is a matter of personal choice.

STRAWBERRY SAUCE

1 quart fresh strawberries, hulled and cut into quarters

¼ cup granulated sugar

SHORTCAKE

2 cups sifted all-purpose flour

¼ cup plus 2 tablespoons granulated sugar

1 tablespoon plus 1 teaspoon baking powder

4 tablespoons cold unsalted butter, cut into bits

½ cup milk

1 large egg

CREAM TOPPING

1 cup heavy cream

2 tablespoons confectioners' sugar

Whole strawberries, for garnish

1. To make the strawberry sauce, in a large bowl, toss the quartered strawberries with the granulated sugar. Cover the sauce and set it aside.

2. Preheat the oven to 425°F. Butter an 8- by 1½-inch layer-cake pan. Dust the pan with flour, shaking out the excess.

3. To make the shortcake, in a food processor, put the flour, granulated sugar, and baking powder. Pulse to mix. Add the butter in three additions, pulsing after each addition. Transfer the mixture to a large bowl.

4. In a small bowl, whisk together the milk and egg. Add this to the flour mixture

and stir briskly, until the dough just holds together.

5. Turn the dough out onto a well-floured surface and knead lightly with floured fingertips 10 times, or until a smooth dough forms. Put the dough in the center of the prepared pan. Using your fingertips, gently spread it evenly, working from the center toward the edges.

6. Bake for 15 to 20 minutes, until golden brown and a toothpick inserted in the center comes out clean. Let the shortcake cool in the pan on a rack for about 10 minutes. Turn out of the pan onto the rack and let it cool completely

7. When shortcake has cooled, make the cream topping. In the chilled small bowl of an electric mixer, at high speed, beat the cream until soft peaks form. Add the confectioners' sugar, beating until stiff peaks just begin to form.

8. To serve, place the shortcake on a serving plate and spread it with the cream filling. Garnish with whole berries. Cut the shortcake into wedges, place on dessert plates, and spoon the strawberry sauce over each serving.

Ripe, juicy strawberries and dollops of cream are spooned over tender shortcake.

STRAWBERRY CREAM PIE WITH ALMOND PASTRY

Makes 8 servings

ALMOND PASTRY

¾ cup slivered almonds

1 cup all-purpose flour

¼ teaspoon ground nutmeg

Pinch of salt

¼ teaspoon almond extract

6 tablespoons cold unsalted
butter, cut into bits

STRAWBERRY FILLING

4 cups fresh strawberries,
halved

2 tablespoons freshly squeezed
lemon juice

⅔ cup sugar

¼ cup cornstarch

CREAM TOPPING

1 cup heavy cream

2 tablespoons almond liqueur

Whole strawberries and
sliced or slivered almonds,
for garnish

1. To make the almond pastry, in a food processor, process the slivered almonds until they are finely ground. Add the flour, nutmeg, and salt and pulse several times, until lightly blended. Add the almond extract.

2. Add the butter alternately with 3 tablespoons of ice water in three additions, pulsing after each addition, until the mixture is crumbly. Continue pulsing until the dough pulls away from the side of the bowl and forms a ball.

3. Shape the dough into a disk, wrap it in plastic, and refrigerate at least 1 hour, or until well chilled.

4. Preheat the oven to 400°F. Butter a 9-inch pie plate. Dust the pie plate with flour, shaking out the excess.

5. Roll the dough on a well-floured surface into a 12-inch round. Carefully fit the dough, which is fragile, into the prepared pie plate. Trim and flute the edge and prick the pastry all over with a fork. Line the pastry with a double

Almond-flavored cream is a sensational match with strawberries.

thickness of foil and fill the foil with dried beans or pie weights.

6. Bake for 20 minutes. Remove the foil and beans and bake for 5 to 7 minutes longer, until golden brown. Transfer the pastry to a rack to cool completely.

7. Meanwhile, make the strawberry filling. In a food processor, put the halved berries and lemon juice. Pulse several times, until the berries are mashed but not pureed. Transfer the mashed berries to a 1-quart glass measure and add enough water to measure 2⅔ cups.

8. In a heavy medium-size saucepan, mix together the sugar and cornstarch. Stir in the mashed strawberries and cook over medium heat, whisking constantly, until the mixture thickens and boils. Cook, whisking, for 2 minutes longer.

9. Pour the filling into a medium-size bowl and press plastic wrap directly onto the surface. Cool to room temperature, about 2 hours. Pour into the cooled pie shell, cover, and refrigerate until the filling is set, about 4 hours.

10. Just before serving, make the cream topping. In the chilled small bowl of an electric mixer, at high speed, beat the cream until soft peaks form. Gradually add the almond liqueur, beating just until stiff peaks form.

11. Spoon the cream topping over the filling in the pie shell. Garnish with whole strawberries and almonds. Refrigerate any leftovers.

Champagne Chestnut Torte
(recipe on page 60)

CHOCOLATE

Thick slices of chocolate cake eaten out of hand on the front porch swing, warm chocolate pudding eagerly licked off the wooden spoon that stirred it, a small finger surreptitiously  dipped into freshly made chocolate batter: For many of us these are among the sweetest of our childhood memories. Nothing envelops or warms or assures quite like the aroma of chocolate ~ unless it is the aroma of chocolate and baking combined. In this chapter the two meet in recipes homey, comforting, elegant, delicious, even sinful. The selection includes cakes, tortes, cookies, and all manner of elaborate confections in between ~ fudgy chocolate-glazed brownies begging to be taken on the next family outing; double-chocolate cream cheese cupcakes perfect for a picnic; and featherlight madeleines just meant for afternoon tea.

CREAM PUFFS WITH CHOCOLATE BAVARIAN CREAM

Makes 8 cream puffs

Made from choux pastry dough, cream puffs are hollow, round shells ~ light, airy, and adaptable to an enticing array of fillings such as whipped cream, Bavarian cream, and pastry cream, making them the perfect way to dress up a dessert table. These cream puffs are filled with a chocolate Bavarian cream ~ ethereal!

CHOUX PASTRY

½ cup milk

7½ tablespoons unsalted butter, cut into bits

1 teaspoon granulated sugar

¾ teaspoon salt

1 cup all-purpose flour

1 cup eggs (4 or 5), well beaten

Confectioners' sugar

CHOCOLATE BAVARIAN CREAM

Four 1-ounce squares semisweet chocolate, coarsely chopped

1 envelope unflavored gelatin

1 cup milk

4 large egg yolks, at room temperature

¼ cup plus 2 tablespoons granulated sugar

1¼ cups heavy cream

1. Preheat the oven to 425°F. Line two baking sheets with parchment paper pressing the corners of the paper to the baking sheets with dabs of butter.

2. To make the choux pastry, in a medium-size heavy saucepan, combine the milk, butter, granulated sugar, and salt with ½ cup of water. Bring to a boil over medium heat, stirring to melt the butter. Remove from the heat.

3. Add the flour and beat vigorously with a wooden spoon until it is blended. Return it to medium heat and cook, beating constantly for 1 minute, or until the dough no longer sticks to the spoon and pulls away from the side of the saucepan. Transfer the mixture to the large bowl of an electric mixer.

4. With the mixer at medium speed, gradually beat in one-third of the beaten eggs, until they are blended. Add the remaining eggs, in two batches, and beat until the dough is smooth and shiny.

5. Spoon the dough into a pastry bag fitted with a ¾-inch plain tip. Pipe the dough into 1½-inch rounds, spaced one inch apart, on the prepared baking sheets. Dust with confectioners' sugar.

6. Bake the cream puffs for 15 minutes. Reduce the oven temperature to 400°F, prop the door open slightly, and bake for 10 to 15 minutes longer, until they are well browned and crisp. Transfer the puffs to a rack and cool completely.

7. Meanwhile, make the chocolate Bavarian cream. Melt the chocolate in the top of a double boiler over barely simmering water. Keeping the chocolate over the water, remove the pan from the heat and stir the chocolate until smooth.

8. While the chocolate melts, soften the gelatin by sprinkling it over ¼ cup of cold water in a small bowl.

9. Pour the milk into a medium-size heavy saucepan and bring it to a boil over medium heat. Remove from the heat.

10. Lightly whisk the egg yolks in a medium-size bowl. Whisk in the granulated sugar and then gradually whisk in the hot milk.

11. Return the mixture to the saucepan. Stirring constantly with a wooden spoon, cook over medium-low heat, until the mixture thickens slightly and registers 165° to 170°F on an instant-read or candy thermometer. Remove from the heat.

12. Immediately whisk in the softened gelatin until it is dissolved and pour the mixture into a large bowl. Stir for 3 minutes to cool it slightly.

13. Remove the chocolate from the double boiler and stir until smooth. Whisk the warm custard, ½ cup at a time, into the chocolate. Return the chocolate custard to the large bowl and refrigerate for 20 minutes, or until partially set.

14. In the chilled small bowl of the mixer, at high speed, whip the cream until it is nearly stiff. With a large rubber spatula, gently fold the whipped cream into the chocolate custard until blended.

15. To assemble, with a serrated knife, split the puffs almost in half horizontally. Pipe or spoon the Bavarian cream into the puffs. Sprinkle the tops with more confectioners' sugar and serve immediately, or refrigerate.

MARCH'S WARM CHOCOLATE CAKE

Makes 6 servings

This recipe comes from the delightful March restaurant in New York City. For the chocolate whipped cream that graces this dessert, the chef uses Ibarra chocolate, a Mexican confection of chocolate, sugar, and cinnamon, but sweet baking chocolate will work just as well. The texture of these mini cakes is similar to that of a baked pudding, with an intense chocolate taste that will satiate any lover of chocolate.

CHOCOLATE CAKES

12 ounces bittersweet chocolate, coarsely chopped

1½ cups (3 sticks) unsalted butter, cut into bits

¾ cup sugar

6 extra-large eggs

6 extra-large egg yolks

¾ cup all-purpose flour

CHOCOLATE WHIPPED CREAM

¾ cup heavy cream

2 ounces sweet chocolate, very finely chopped or grated (preferably Mexican Ibarra chocolate)

Chocolate sails and flower petals, for garnish (optional)

1. Preheat the oven to 375°F. Spray six 1-cup nonstick fluted mini-tube pan cups generously with nonstick cooking spray.

2. To make the chocolate cakes, in the top of a double boiler, over barely simmering water, melt the bittersweet chocolate and butter, stirring often. Remove from the heat and let the chocolate cool to room temperature.

3. In the large bowl of an electric mixer, at high speed, beat the sugar, eggs, and egg yolks until they are thick, creamy, and lemon-colored, about 6 minutes.

4. Sift the flour evenly over the beaten eggs and then pour in the chocolate. With the mixer at low speed, beat until blended, scraping the side of the bowl constantly. Increase the mixer speed to medium-high and beat for 10 minutes.

5. Pour the batter into the prepared pans, filling the cups full to the rim (cover

An extra burst of chocolate flavor is released when served warm.

the center stem of the molds). Place the pans on a baking sheet.

6. Bake for 20 minutes, or until slight cracks appear. Cool the cakes for 1 hour.

7. Meanwhile, make the chocolate whipped cream. In the small bowl of the mixer, at high speed, beat the cream just until soft peaks form. By hand, fold in the sweet chocolate. Refrigerate the cream until you are ready to serve.

8. Carefully run a knife around the edge of each pan to loosen the cakes and turn them out onto a work surface. Place the warm cakes on dessert plates. Garnish with the chocolate whipped cream, chocolate sails, and flower petals, and serve.

FLOURLESS CHOCOLATE CAKE

Makes 12 to 14 servings

This cake is also known as a fallen soufflé cake since both desserts are prepared with the same ingredients. Don't worry when it falls in the center as it cools ~ there isn't any flour to give it structure. This very chocolatey cake should be served in thin slices accompanied by unsweetened softly whipped cream.

1⅓ cups granulated sugar

1 cup (2 sticks) unsalted butter, cut into bits

Six 1-ounce squares semisweet chocolate, coarsely chopped

Six 1-ounce squares unsweetened chocolate, coarsely chopped

5 large eggs, at room temperature

Confectioners' sugar, for garnish

1. In a small heavy saucepan, stir together 1 cup of the granulated sugar with ½ cup of water. Bring to a boil over medium-high heat, stirring to dissolve the sugar. Brush down the side of the pan with a pastry brush dipped in cold water. Boil the syrup, without stirring, for 4 minutes. Remove from the heat and let cool to room temperature. (The syrup may crystallize during cooling.)

2. In the top of a double boiler, over barely simmering water, melt the butter and both chocolates, stirring often. Remove from the heat and stir the chocolate mixture until it is smooth. Cool the chocolate to room temperature.

3. Preheat the oven to 350°F. Butter a 9- by 2-inch layer-cake pan. Line the pan bottom with parchment paper cut to fit and butter the paper. Dust the pan with flour, shaking out the excess.

4. In the large bowl of an electric mixer, at high speed, beat the eggs and the remaining ⅓ cup of sugar for about 10 minutes, or until the mixture is light and

A single layer of pure decadence: so rich, you can serve it in slivers.

lemon-colored, has tripled in volume, and forms a slowly dissolving ribbon.

5. Slowly pour in the cooled sugar syrup, beating constantly. With a large rubber spatula, gradually fold in the chocolate mixture until it is blended.

6. Scrape the batter into the prepared pan. Place the cake pan in a shallow baking pan and pour hot water around the cake pan to a depth of 1 inch.

7. Bake for 1 hour and 15 minutes. A toothpick inserted into the center will not come out clean. The cake will be very moist inside with a slight crust on top. Remove the cake pan from the water bath and place it on a rack. Let the cake cool to room temperature. (The cake will rise high during baking, then settle and crack during cooling.) Loosely cover the cake and refrigerate overnight.

8. Run a warm knife around the edge of the pan to loosen the cake. Gently heat the pan bottom by placing it in hot water for 1 to 2 minutes, until warm to the touch. Tap the pan sharply on the counter and invert the cake onto a flat baking sheet. (If it does not release, repeat the process.) Peel off the paper and invert the cake, top-side up, onto a serving plate.

9. Refrigerate until 30 minutes before serving. Dust with confectioners' sugar.

There's nothing like super-brownies: moist, chewy, and oh so chocolaty!

BROWNIE TORTE

Makes 12 servings

This is the the ultimate brownie for adults only ~ two layers high, spiked with bourbon, studded with pecans, and covered with a soft cocoa icing. Chocolate sprinkles dress up the sides of the torte and pecan halves complete the look.

BROWNIE TORTE

2 cups sifted all-purpose flour

2 teaspoons baking powder

½ teaspoon salt

½ cup (1 stick) unsalted butter, at room temperature

2 cups granulated sugar

Four 1-ounce squares unsweetened chocolate, melted and cooled

2 large eggs, separated and yolks well beaten

2 tablespoons bourbon

1 teaspoon vanilla extract

½ cup milk

1 cup chopped pecans

CHOCOLATE ICING

½ cup (1 stick) plus 2 tablespoons unsalted butter, at room temperature

¾ cup sifted unsweetened cocoa powder

2 tablespoons bourbon

2 tablespoons light corn syrup

½ teaspoon salt

1 pound box confectioners' sugar, sifted

3 tablespoons hot milk

Chocolate sprinkles and pecan halves, for garnish

1. Preheat the oven to 350°F. Butter two 9-inch layer-cake pans. Line the pan bottoms with waxed paper cut to fit and butter the paper. Dust the pans with flour, shaking out the excess.

2. To make the brownie torte, sift the flour, baking powder, and salt three times.

3. In the large bowl of an electric mixer, at high speed, beat the butter until it is creamy. Gradually add the granulated sugar, beating until the mixture is light and fluffy, scraping the side of the bowl often. Beat in the melted chocolate.

4. Reduce the mixer speed to medium and beat in the egg yolks, bourbon, and vanilla until the mixture is smooth.

5. Reduce the mixer speed to low and stir in the flour mixture in three additions, alternately with the milk, mixing until just blended after each addition, and beginning and ending with the flour. Fold in the pecans.

6. Wash the beaters. In the medium-size bowl of the mixer, at high speed, beat the egg whites until stiff peaks form when the beaters are lifted.

7. Stir a spoonful of the beaten egg whites into the batter to lighten it. Then, with a large rubber spatula, gently fold in the remaining whites. (The batter will be very thick.) Spread the batter evenly in the prepared pans.

8. Bake for 35 minutes, or until the cakes begin to pull away from the sides of the pans. (They will rise and then settle during baking, forming a cracked crust.)

9. Cool the cakes in their pans on racks for 10 minutes. Loosen the cake edges with a thin metal spatula and turn the cakes out of the pans onto the racks. Peel off the paper and let the cakes cool completely.

10. To make the chocolate icing, in the large bowl of the mixer, at medium speed, beat the butter, cocoa, bourbon, corn syrup, and salt, until they are smooth, scraping down the side of the bowl.

11. Reduce the mixer speed to low and gradually beat in the confectioners' sugar alternately with the hot milk, a few drops at a time, until the icing is smooth. Increase the mixer speed to high and beat the icing until it is fluffy.

12. Place one of the cake layers on a serving plate. Spread it with some of the icing and place the second cake layer on top. Ice the top and sides of the torte, swirling the frosting decoratively with a narrow metal spatula. Spoon any remaining frosting into a pastry bag fitted with a star tip and pipe rosettes along the top edge of the cake. Garnish the cake sides with chocolate sprinkles, arrange pecan halves on the cake plate along the base of the cake, and serve.

CHOCOLATE MADELEINES

Makes 12 madeleines

¼ cup sifted all-purpose flour

¼ cup unsweetened cocoa
   powder

½ teaspoon baking powder

Pinch of salt

1 teaspoon instant coffee
   crystals

4 tablespoons unsalted butter,
   at room temperature

¼ cup granulated sugar

1 teaspoon brandy

½ teaspoon vanilla extract

1 large egg, at room
   temperature

2 large egg yolks, at room
   temperature

Confectioners' sugar,
   for garnish

1. Preheat the oven to 375°F. Brush twelve madeleine pan molds with soft butter, evenly coating each mold.

2. Sift the flour, cocoa powder, baking powder, and salt into a large bowl. Stir in the coffee crystals.

3. In the large bowl of an electric mixer, at medium speed, beat the butter until it is creamy. Add the granulated sugar, brandy, and vanilla and beat until the mixture is well blended, scraping down the side of the bowl often.

4. Beat in the whole egg and egg yolks until thoroughly incorporated. (The mixture will look curdled.)

5. Reduce the mixer speed to low and beat in the flour mixture just until it is blended. (Do not overmix.)

6. Spoon a rounded tablespoon of the madeleine batter into each prepared mold. Place the filled madeleine pan on a baking sheet.

7. Bake for 12 minutes, or until a toothpick inserted in the center comes out clean. Cool in the pan for 1 minute. Carefully loosen the madeleines with a small knife and turn them out onto a rack to cool completely.

8. Dust the madeleines with confectioners' sugar before serving.

SACHER TORTE

Makes 8 Servings

Austrian pastry chef Franz Sacher deserves all the credit for this cocoa-based torte, filled with tangy apricot preserves and enrobed in chocolate. The word *Sacher* written in chocolate across the torte is the finishing touch. In Vienna, Sacher Torte is a must at the Sacher Hotel and at Demel's pastry shop, where it is always served *mit schlag* ("with whipped cream").

TORTE

2⅓ cups sifted cake flour

1 cup Dutch-process cocoa

1½ teaspoons salt

1 teaspoon baking powder

¾ cup (1½ sticks) plus 2 tablespoons unsalted butter, at room temperature

2 cups sugar

6 large eggs, at room temperature

⅓ cup lukewarm milk

⅓ to ½ cup Sugar Syrup (page 194)

¾ cup apricot preserves, melted and strained

GANACHE

½ cup heavy cream

½ cup milk

10 ounces bittersweet chocolate, finely chopped

1. Preheat the oven to 300°F. Butter a 9-inch springform pan. Line the pan bottom with waxed paper cut to fit and butter the paper. Dust the pan with flour, shaking out the excess.
2. To make the torte, sift together the flour, cocoa, salt, and baking powder.
3. In the large bowl of an electric mixer, at high speed, beat the butter until it is creamy. Gradually add the sugar and beat until it is light and fluffy.
4. Reduce the mixer speed to medium and beat in the eggs, one at a time, beating well after each addition.
5. Reduce the mixer speed to low. Add the flour in three additions, alternately

A sweeter, more cake-like version of the traditional dense torte.

with the lukewarm milk, mixing just until blended after each addition, and beginning and ending with the flour.

6. Pour the batter into the prepared pan. Bake for 1 to 1¼ hours, until the center of the cake is just firm to the touch. Let the cake cool completely in the pan on a rack. Run a thin metal spatula around the edge of the pan to loosen the cake and remove the pan sides. Invert the cake onto the rack. Loosen and remove the pan bottom, peel off the paper, and turn the cake top side up.

7. Meanwhile, make the ganache. In a heavy medium-size saucepan, bring the cream and milk to a boil over medium heat. Reduce the heat to low and gradually add the chocolate, stirring until the chocolate is melted and the mixture is smooth. Pour the ganache into a large bowl and let it cool to tepid. (Do not allow the ganache to cool completely or it will be difficult to spread.)

8. With a long serrated knife, split the cake in half horizontally. Brush the cut sides of the cake with just enough of the sugar syrup to moisten the layers evenly.

9. With a thin metal spatula, evenly spread the apricot preserves on the cut side of the bottom cake layer. Place the top layer, cut-side down, over the bottom layer and place the cake on a rack set over a jelly-roll pan.

10. Slowly pour the ganache over the cake, smoothing the top and sides with a thin metal spatula and letting the excess drip onto the jelly-roll pan. Allow the ganache to set completely and then transfer the cake to a serving plate. Refrigerate any leftovers.

Storied Sweets: Demel's Old Vienna

No trip to Vienna is complete without a visit to Demel's, the legendary pastry shop and café that has been tempting—and satisfying—chocolate lovers since the late 1800's. Though Demel's offers a choice of over 200 treats—from lebkuchen, the European Christmas cookies fabled to bring good fortune, to kugelhupf, the buttery coffee cake whose origins date from the 1500's—it is their Sacher Torte that is famous world-wide. As sumptuous as a Viennese waltz, this chocolate cake is coated with apricot preserves before being enrobed in a rich chocolate ganache as dark as the Black Forest. This torte travels beautifully, as does Demel's selection of bon-bons and chocolates—all packaged in candy boxes so magnificently printed with Victorian era designs, they can only be described as "heirloom quality".

True indulgence awaits the patron who lingers over dessert in Demel's graceful belle époque building, with its fin-de-siècle European mouldings, marble tables, tile floors, and tall glittering mirrors. Waitresses in traditional black and white uniforms encourage dessert in the extravagant Demel style. At least two or three slices of rich cake "mit schlag" (with sweetened whipped cream), accompanied by a comforting cup of tea, coffee, or hot chocolate keep guests going until the next scrumptious foray.

The modest name for their Coffee Nut Cake doesn't begin to hint at the splendors of this dazzling hazelnut layer cake slathered with a dense coffee cream filling and frosting.

A delicious dilemma at Demel's: which torte to taste?

For anyone wishing to cleanse the palate between cake courses, there are refreshing Demel fruit tarts—fresh blueberries, cherries, and strawberries all wrapped in shells of rich buttery melt-in-your-mouth pie crust.

After more than one hundred years, Demel's tradition of hospitality continues to burn brightly—in large part, we are told, due to the efforts of the Demel family women. One leisurely stop at this glorious mecca of culinary excellence promises to sweeten any future stay in the fine old city of Vienna.

TRUFFLE CAKE

Makes 12 servings

CAKE

5 large eggs, separated

½ cup granulated sugar

¼ cup confectioners' sugar

Two and one-quarter 1-ounce
squares semisweet chocolate,
melted and cooled

1¼ cups finely ground
blanched almonds

⅓ cup all-purpose flour

GANACHE

3⅓ cups heavy cream

12 ounces semisweet
chocolate, finely chopped

Chocolate sprinkles and
chocolate curls made from a
4-ounce bar of semisweet
chocolate, for garnish

1. Preheat the oven to 325°F. Butter a 9-inch springform pan. Line the bottom of the pan with waxed paper or parchment paper cut to fit and butter the paper. Dust the pan with flour, shaking out the excess.

2. To make the cake, in the large bowl of an electric mixer, at high speed, beat the egg whites until soft peaks form. Add ¼ cup of the granulated sugar and beat until stiff peaks form when the beaters are lifted. Gently pour the beaten whites into a large bowl, being careful not to deflate them.

3. Put the egg yolks into the same mixer bowl and beat at high speed, until they are just broken up. (There is no need to wash the bowl or beaters.) Gradually add the remaining ¼ cup of granulated sugar and the confectioners' sugar, beating until the mixture is light and fluffy. Beat in the melted chocolate.

4. In a small bowl, stir together the ground almonds and flour.

5. By hand, gently stir the flour mixture into the egg yolks, a little at a time, until just mixed. Stir a quarter of the whites into the yolk mixture. Then, with a large rubber spatula, gently but thoroughly fold in the remaining whites. Pour the batter into the prepared pan and smooth the top.

6. Bake for 35 to 40 minutes, until the cake feels firm when it is gently pressed in

the center. Let the cake cool in the pan on a rack for 5 minutes. Run a thin metal spatula around the edge of the pan to loosen the cake and remove the pan sides. Let the cake cool completely on the rack.

7. To make the ganache, in a large heavy saucepan, bring the cream to a simmer over medium heat. Add the bittersweet chocolate, a little at a time, stirring until the chocolate is melted and the ganache is smooth. Transfer to the large bowl of the mixer and chill, stirring occasionally, for 20 to 30 minutes, until it is cold and thickened. Then, with the mixer at high speed, beat the ganache until it holds soft peaks when the beaters are lifted.

8. Remove the pan bottom from the cake and peel off the paper. Using a long serrated knife, split the cake horizontally into three layers and place the bottom layer on a serving plate. Spread a thin layer of the ganache on the bottom layer, top with the second layer, and spread it with ganache. Add the third layer, cut side down. Spread a thin layer of ganache on the top and sides of the cake.

9. Spoon half of the remaining ganache into a pastry bag fitted with a large star tip. Pipe twelve rosettes along the top edge of the cake and refrigerate.

10. To make the chocolate truffles, spoon the remaining ganache into the pastry bag and pipe twelve marble-size mounds on a waxed paper–lined baking sheet. Freeze the truffles until they are firm. Roll each truffle into a ball and coat them with chocolate sprinkles. Top each rosette with a truffle and then decorate the top of the cake with chocolate curls. Refrigerate any leftovers.

Easy-to-make and impressive: a layered sponge iced with truffles.

CHAMPAGNE CHESTNUT TORTE

(PHOTOGRAPH ON PAGE 42)

Makes 12 servings

Blanc de Noir, the preferred Champagne for this torte, is made from the Pinot Noir grape. The grape skins are left in contact with the grape juice just long enough to lend a delicate pinkish apricot blush to the Champagne.

CAKE

1 pound semisweet chocolate, coarsely chopped

½ cup Champagne, preferably Blanc de Noir

One 15½-ounce can unsweetened chestnut puree

½ cup (1 stick) unsalted butter, at room temperature

⅔ cup heavy cream

1½ cups granulated sugar

½ cup all-purpose flour

Pinch of salt

6 large eggs, at room temperature

CHOCOLATE CREAM

2½ ounces white chocolate, coarsely chopped

Two and a half 1-ounce squares semisweet chocolate, coarsely chopped

2 cups heavy cream

¼ cup Champagne, preferably Blanc de Noir

¼ cup confectioners' sugar

Confectioners' sugar and mint sprigs, for garnish

1. Preheat the oven to 350°F. Butter a 10-inch springform pan. Line the bottom of the pan with waxed paper or parchment paper cut to fit and butter the paper. Dust the pan with flour, shaking out the excess.

2. To make the cake, in the top of a double boiler, over hot but not simmering water, melt the semisweet chocolate with the Champagne. Remove from the heat and stir until the mixture is smooth. Let cool to room temperature.

3. In the large bowl of an electric mixer, at medium speed, beat the chestnut puree, butter, and cream until the mixture is blended and smooth. Gradually

beat in the melted chocolate and then the granulated sugar.

4. Add the flour and salt and mix until well blended. Add the eggs, one at a time, beating well after each addition. Pour the batter into the prepared pan.

5. Bake for 1 hour and 20 to 30 minutes, until puffed and a toothpick inserted in the center comes out clean. (The surface of the cake will have cracks.)

6. Cool the cake in the pan on a rack for 10 minutes. Run a thin metal spatula around the edge of the pan to loosen the cake and remove the pan sides. Invert the cake onto the rack. Loosen and remove the pan bottom, and peel off the paper. Turn the cake top side up and let it cool completely.

7. Dust the cooled cake with confectioners' sugar and transfer it to a serving plate.

8. To make the chocolate whipped cream, place the large bowl and the beaters of the mixer in the refrigerator to chill.

9. In two separate double boilers (or small bowls set over saucepans), melt the chocolates separately over barely simmering water, stirring frequently, until they are smooth. Remove the pans from the heat, letting the chocolate continue to sit over the hot water.

10. Whip the cream in the chilled bowl, at high speed, until soft peaks form. Gradually beat in the Champagne and the confectioners' sugar until the cream is moderately stiff. Transfer half of the whipped cream into another bowl.

11. Remove the semisweet chocolate from the water and cool for 3 minutes. Quickly stir about ½ cup of the cream into the semisweet chocolate. Then with a large rubber spatula, quickly fold the chocolate mixture into remaining whipped cream in that bowl until blended. (Work quickly so the chocolate doesn't harden when it comes in contact with the cold cream.)

12. Repeat the process with the white chocolate and the remaining bowl of whipped cream. (Use the chocolate creams right away.)

13. Fill a pastry bag, fitted with a large star tip, with the white-chocolate cream and pipe rosettes along the edge of the cake. Then fill the bag with the dark chocolate cream and pipe additional rosettes on the cake. Garnish the cake with mint sprigs, and serve. Refrigerate any leftovers.

ALMOND FUDGE CAKE

Makes 10 servings

CAKE

Half an 8-ounce can almond
  paste

1¾ cups self-rising flour

2 tablespoons unsweetened
  cocoa powder

1 teaspoon ground cinnamon

¼ teaspoon ground cloves

¾ cup (1½ sticks) unsalted
  butter, at room temperature

¾ cup plus 2 tablespoons
  superfine sugar

1 teaspoon vanilla extract

3 large eggs, at room
  temperature, lightly beaten

½ cup milk

¾ cup slivered almonds,
  toasted

TOPPING

⅔ cup packed light or dark
  brown sugar

4 tablespoons unsalted butter

1 tablespoon heavy cream

¼ cup slivered almonds,
  toasted

1. Preheat the oven to 350°F. Butter an 8- by 3-inch layer-cake pan. Line the pan bottom with waxed paper or parchment paper cut to fit and butter the paper. Dust the pan with flour, shaking out the excess.

2. To make the cake, roll the almond paste between two sheets of waxed paper into an 8-inch round.

3. In a medium-size bowl, stir together the flour, cocoa, cinnamon, and cloves.

4. In the large bowl of an electric mixer, at high speed, beat the butter, superfine sugar, and vanilla until light and fluffy. Reduce the mixer speed to medium and beat in the eggs, one-third at a time, beating well after each addition.

5. Reduce the mixer speed to low and add the flour mixture in two additions, alternately with the milk, mixing just until blended after each addition, and beginning and ending with the flour. Fold in the almonds.

6. Spoon half of the batter into the prepared pan. Top with the round of almond paste and spread the remaining batter evenly over the top.

The flavor of toasted almonds infuses a cocoa and spice layer cake.

7. Bake for 1 hour, or until a toothpick inserted in the center comes out clean. Let the cake cool in the pan on a rack for 10 minutes. Run a thin metal spatula around the edge of the pan to loosen the cake and invert it onto the rack. Peel off the paper and set the rack on a jelly-roll pan. Cool the cake completely.

8. To make the topping, in a small heavy saucepan, place the brown sugar, butter, and the cream. Bring to a boil over medium heat, stirring frequently, until the mixture is well blended and smooth. Remove from the heat.

9. Stir the almonds into the topping and pour it over the cooled cake. Let the cake stand for about 10 minutes, or until the topping is set. Transfer the cake to a serving plate. Refrigerate any leftovers.

Nut Coffeecake With Apricot Filling
(recipe on page 66)

COFFEE

From almost the first time we experience our first sip of coffee, it becomes a lifetime indulgence ~ warming, bracing, comforting, the ideal way to begin and end each day, and perhaps to punctuate special times in between. And as for coffee and cake ~ what could be a more perfect match? Whether you're sipping brewed coffee, latte, cappuccino, or espresso, a bit of sweet always seems called for: a coffeecake, studded with pumpkin and fresh cranberries, a firm-textured apple spice cake, heady with the fragrance of nutmeg, and buttery ginger-scented burnt sugar cookies. Here are also crisp biscotti, made for the discreet pleasure of dunking; fragile shortbread, beloved since childhood, all grown up when paired with a gentle latte; light-as-air meringues; and cardamom-scented yeast breads guaranteed to warm just about any moment of the day.

NUT COFFEECAKE WITH APRICOT FILLING

(Photograph on page 64)

Makes 8 servings

½ cup coarsely ground
zwieback or rusk crumbs,
plus extra crumbs for the pan

1¼ cups skinned and finely
ground hazelnuts
(1⅔ cups whole nuts)

2 teaspoons baking powder

3 large eggs, at room
temperature

¾ cup granulated sugar

½ cup (1 stick) unsalted butter,
melted and cooled

⅔ cup apricot jam

Confectioners' sugar, for
garnish

1. Preheat the oven to 350°F. Butter an 8- by 1½-inch layer-cake pan. Dust the pan with the extra zwieback crumbs.

2. In a small bowl, stir together the zwieback crumbs, ground hazelnuts, and the baking powder.

3. In the large bowl of an electric mixer, at high speed, beat the eggs and granulated sugar until light and pale in color, about 6 minutes.

4. Reduce the mixer speed to medium and gradually beat in the melted butter. By hand, stir in the crumb mixture in three additions, stirring just until blended. Pour half of the batter into the prepared pan.

5. Bake for 15 minutes. Remove the cake from the oven. Spoon small dollops of the apricot jam all over the surface of the cake and spread them evenly. Pour the remaining batter over the jam layer. (The pan will seem very full.)

6. Bake for 25 to 30 minutes longer, until the cake pulls away from the side of the pan and the top springs back when lightly touched.

7. Let the cake cool completely in the pan on a rack. Run a thin metal spatula around the edge of the pan to loosen the cake. Carefully turn the cake out onto a serving plate. Sift confectioners' sugar over the top of cake just before serving.

CHERRY NUTBREAD

Makes 1 loaf cake

The dried tart red cherries used in this cake are much in vogue today. Look for them in gourmet food stores, or purchase them by mail.

3 ounces dried pitted tart red cherries (about ½ cup)

1 tablespoon cherry brandy

2 cups all-purpose flour

1 cup sugar

1 tablespoon baking powder

Pinch of salt

¼ cup solid white vegetable shortening

½ cup milk

2 large eggs, at room temperature

1 tablespoon grated orange zest

¼ cup freshly squeezed orange juice

½ cup chopped walnuts

1. Preheat the oven to 350°F. Butter an 8½- by 4½- by 2½-inch loaf pan. Line the bottom of the pan with waxed paper cut to fit and butter the paper. Dust the pan with flour, shaking out the excess.

2. In a small bowl, toss the dried cherries with the brandy.

3. Sift the flour, sugar, baking powder, and salt into a large bowl. With a pastry blender or two knives, cut in the shortening until the mixture forms a coarse meal.

4. Make a well in the center of the dry ingredients. Add the milk, eggs, and orange zest and juice, stirring with a fork until well blended. Fold in the soaked cherry mixture and the walnuts. Pour the batter into the prepared pan.

5. Bake for 60 to 65 minutes, until a toothpick inserted in the center comes out clean.

6. Let the cake cool in its pan on a rack for 10 minutes. Run a thin metal spatula around the edges to loosen the cake and turn the cake out onto a rack. Peel off the paper and let the cake cool completely. Cut into thin slices and serve.

PUMPKIN-CRANBERRY COFFEECAKE

Makes 12 to 16 servings

This festive coffeecake is the only one we've ever seen that features pumpkin and cranberries. Coffeecakes are good desserts for low-key meals like Sunday supper, and this one is a terrific picnic traveler.

2¼ cups all-purpose flour

1 tablespoon pumpkin-pie spice

1 teaspoon baking soda

½ teaspoon salt

2 large eggs, at room temperature

2 cups granulated sugar

1 cup canned solid-pack pumpkin puree

½ cup vegetable oil

1 cup cranberries, coarsely chopped

Granulated sugar, for garnish

1. Preheat the oven to 350°F. Butter an 8-cup ring mold or other decorative mold. Dust the pan with flour, shaking out the excess.

2. In a large bowl, stir together the flour, pumpkin-pie spice, baking soda, and salt.

3. In the medium-size bowl of an electric mixer, at medium speed, beat the eggs until they are foamy. Beat in the granulated sugar, pumpkin puree, and oil until well blended. Add the pumpkin mixture to the flour mixture and stir just until a batter forms. (Do not overmix.) Gently fold in the cranberries.

4. Spread the batter evenly in the prepared pan and place on a baking sheet.

5. Bake for 50 minutes, or until a toothpick inserted in the center comes out clean. Let the cake cool in the pan on a rack for 10 minutes. Run a thin metal spatula around the edge of the mold to loosen the cake and turn the cake out onto the rack to cool completely.

6. Sprinkle the cake with granulated sugar before serving.

Two harvest-time fruits mingle in a simple, unadorned cake.

COFFEE NUT TORTE

Makes 12 servings

TORTE

¾ cup (1½ sticks) unsalted
  butter, at room temperature

⅔ cup confectioners' sugar

9 large eggs, separated

1 teaspoon grated lemon zest

1 teaspoon vanilla extract

1¾ cups hazelnuts, skinned and
  finely ground (7 ounces)

½ cup fresh white bread crumbs
  or cake crumbs (page 86)

Pinch of salt

½ cup granulated sugar

CHOCOLATE CREAM

1 cup brewed espresso

1 cup milk

¼ cup granulated sugar

½ teaspoon vanilla extract

Pinch of salt

1 ounce vanilla instant pudding
  mix (about ¼ cup)

2 large egg yolks

1 envelope unflavored gelatin

Three and one half 1-ounce
  squares semisweet
  chocolate, finely chopped

¾ cup heavy cream

Chocolate coffee beans and
  ground nuts, for garnish

1. Preheat the oven to 350°F. Butter a 9-inch springform pan. Line the bottom of the pan with waxed paper or parchment paper cut to fit and butter the paper. Dust the pan with flour, shaking out the excess.

2. To make the torte, in the large bowl of an electric mixer, at medium-high speed, beat the butter until it is creamy. Gradually add the confectioners' sugar and beat until light and fluffy. Add the egg yolks, one at a time, beating well after each addition. Beat in the lemon zest and vanilla.

3. In a medium-size bowl, stir together the nuts and bread crumbs. By hand, stir the crumbs into the butter mixture, stirring just until blended. Scrape into a large bowl and wash the mixer bowl and beaters.

4. Put the egg whites and salt into the large mixer bowl. Beat at high speed until the egg whites form soft peaks. Gradually beat in the granulated sugar until stiff peaks form when the beaters are lifted. Fold a big spoonful of the beaten egg

whites into the cake batter using a large rubber spatula, then gently but thoroughly fold in the remaining egg whites.

5. Pour the batter into the prepared pan and smooth the surface. Bake for 45 to 50 minutes, until the top feels firm when gently pressed in the center. Let the cake cool completely in the pan on a rack. Run a thin metal spatula around the edge of the cake to loosen it and remove the pan sides. Invert the cake onto the rack, remove the pan bottom, and peel off the paper. Turn the cake top side up.

6. To make the chocolate cream, in a heavy medium-size saucepan, stir together the espresso, ½ cup of the milk, the granulated sugar, vanilla, and salt. Bring to a boil over medium heat, stirring frequently. Remove from the heat.

7. In a medium-size bowl, whisk together the remaining ½ cup of milk and the pudding mix until smooth. Whisk in the egg yolks. Gradually whisk in ½ cup of the hot espresso mixture, then whisk this mixture back into the remaining espresso mixture in the saucepan.

8. Place the saucepan over medium-low heat. Cook, stirring constantly with a wooden spoon, until the custard is slightly thickened. Scrape into a large bowl.

9. In a small bowl, sprinkle the gelatin over ¼ cup of cold water and let it stand for 5 minutes to soften. Stir the gelatin into the warm custard until blended.

10. Add the chocolate to the custard and stir until it is smooth and melted. Cover and chill for 20 minutes. (Do not let the custard set.)

11. In the chilled small bowl of the mixer, at high speed, beat the cream until soft peaks form. With a large rubber spatula, fold the cream into the custard and chill the chocolate cream for 20 minutes.

12. With a long serrated knife, slice the cake horizontally into three layers. Place the bottom cake layer on a serving plate and spread with a thin layer of the chocolate cream. Top with another cake layer and more cream. Put the top layer over the filled layers and spread the top and sides thinly with some of the remaining cream. Chill the cake and the remaining chocolate cream for 30 minutes.

13. Transfer the chocolate cream to a pastry bag fitted with a large star tip and pipe rosettes on top of the cake. Place a coffee bean in the center of each rosette and sprinkle the cake sides with ground nuts. Keep the cake refrigerated until you are ready to serve. Refrigerate any leftovers.

CARDAMOM COFFEE BREADS

Makes 1 braided loaf and 1 ring loaf

This recipe makes a cardamom-scented yeast dough which is divided and shaped to make two different breads ~ a braided loaf and a sweet, sticky, cinnamon ring. You will need a heavy-duty standing electric mixer with a paddle and a dough hook attachment to prepare this dough, or make it by hand, a portable mixer just isn't strong enough.

BASIC DOUGH

2 envelopes active dry yeast

2½ cups lukewarm milk (95° to 110°F)

8 cups all-purpose flour, plus additional flour for kneading and shaping

1 cup granulated sugar

¾ cup (1½ sticks) unsalted butter, melted and cooled

1 large egg, at room temperature

15 cardamom pods, crushed, or 1 teaspoon ground cardamom

½ teaspoon salt

COFFEE BRAID

1 large egg, lightly beaten

Coarse-grained sugar and chopped almonds, for garnish

CINNAMON RING

2 tablespoons unsalted butter, melted

½ cup granulated sugar

1 teaspoon ground cinnamon

1. To make the basic dough, in a small bowl, dissolve the yeast in ½ cup of the lukewarm milk. Let the yeast stand for about 10 minutes, or until it is foamy.

2. In the large bowl of an electric mixer, with the paddle attachment, combine 2 cups of the flour, the granulated sugar, the remaining 2 cups of milk, the butter, egg, cardamom, salt, and the yeast mixture. Beat at medium speed for 2 minutes.

3. Add 3 more cups of the flour, 1 cup at a time, beating until blended after each addition. Increase the mixer speed to high and beat for 2 minutes longer. With the dough hook or by hand, stir in the remaining 3 cups of flour to make a moderately soft dough. Turn the dough into a large buttered bowl and turn it once to coat the top of the dough with butter.

4. Cover the dough with a tea towel and let it rise in a warm place, away from drafts, until it is doubled in volume, about 1¼ hours.

5. Punch the dough down. Knead the dough on a lightly floured surface until it is smooth and elastic, about 15 minutes, adding additional flour, a little at a time as needed. (The dough is quite soft and sticky—using a dough scraper makes kneading easier.) If you prefer, return the dough to the mixer bowl and knead using the dough hook, for 7 to 8 minutes, until the dough is smooth.

6. Divide the dough in half. Cover each piece of dough with a tea towel and allow it to rest for 10 minutes. Butter two heavy baking sheets.

7. To make the coffee braid, cut one piece of the dough into three equal portions. With lightly floured hands, and working on a floured board, roll each piece of dough into a rope about 15 inches long, tapering them at the ends.

8. Put the ropes diagonally on one of the prepared baking sheets, placing the ropes about 1½ inches apart. Pinch the three ropes together at one end and begin braiding, pulling gently on the ropes as you braid. Pinch the ends of the dough braid together, tucking them under the loaf.

9. Cover the braid with a tea towel and let it rise in a warm place until it is doubled in volume, about 30 minutes.

10. Preheat the oven to 375°F. While the coffee braid is rising, make the cinnamon ring. Roll the remaining piece of dough on a well-floured surface into an 18- by 10-inch rectangle. Brush with the melted butter. In a small bowl, com-

Coffee at Lady Mendl's

Finding an inn tucked in New York City's Gramercy Park neighborhood is just the first of many surprises awaiting visitors to Naomi Blumenthal's The Inn at Irving Place. A turn of the doorknob and you enter a nineteenth-century enclave of peace and perfection. In a restoration, Naomi opened up two adjoining 1834 brownstone buildings to make an intimate twelve-room inn. The sweeping parlors, guest suites, and nooks and crannies were so faithfully decorated in the Victorian mode that a vivid portrait of daily life over a century ago permeates the space.

Pots of coffee inspire long chats at Lady Mendl's.

Every room is a gem, but perhaps the one that sparkles the brightest of all is the tea salon Lady Mendl's, named in honor of Elsie de Wolfe. An influential American designer, Miss de Wolfe lived across the street. After her marriage to Sir Charles Mendl, she entered into English society and acquired the title so happily shared by her neighboring tearoom.

As well mannered as a calling card, Lady Mendl's is a study in comfort. Deep upholstered armchairs and sofas wrap their plump arms around guests, defying stress and busyness.

Bouquets of fresh flowers mingle their scents with sweet cakes and pastries. Soft lighting and muted colorings whisper softly as one prepares to consider the delicious options coffee time offers. But there's no written menu. A believer in providing her guests with only the best, Naomi varies her choices so constantly that waiters recite the tempting daily selections.

On a spring afternoon, visitors might start to relax with a savory course such as petit pain (or little roll) sandwiched with grilled pears, cambozola cheese, and watercress. Those in search of sweeter fare may revel in the traditional assortment of rich, creamy Victorian fruit tarts. But, for a truly extraordinary experience, one can settle back into a damask covered armchair and spend a "chocolate hour" sampling miniature chocolates, or savor Lady Mendl's spectacularly elegant dark chocolate boîte filled with raspberries, meant to be devoured in its entirety.

As New York shades of night begin to fall and parlor lamps are lit, a glow of contentment spreads across Lady Mendl's. It's been such a wonderful visit, perhaps there's room for just one more cup of coffee?

bine the granulated sugar and the cinnamon and sprinkle evenly over the dough. Starting with one long side, roll up the dough jelly-roll fashion.

11. Carefully transfer the dough to the second baking sheet with the seam on the bottom. Form the roll into a circle, moisten the ends, and pinch the ends together to seal.

12. With scissors held at an angle, cut the roll at 1-inch intervals, leaving ½ inch of the roll intact (uncut) at the bottom. Fan the cuts alternately to the right, then to the left around the ring. Cover the ring loosely with plastic wrap and let the ring rise in a warm place until it is doubled in volume, about 30 minutes.

13. Meanwhile, gently brush the coffee braid with some of the beaten egg. Sprinkle with coarse sugar and chopped almonds. Bake for 25 to 30 minutes, until the bread is golden brown and sounds hollow when tapped on the bottom. Transfer the coffee braid to a rack to cool.

14. When the cinnamon ring has risen, gently brush it with beaten egg. Bake for 20 to 25 minutes. With two pancake turners, transfer the ring to a rack to cool.

Sweet Spices

Cinnamon, cardamom, allspice, cloves, mace, and nutmeg~the sweet spices have always been prized by cooks because of the enticing flavors and aromas they impart to baked goods such as cakes, pies, tortes, and yeast breads. A spice's pungency is dependent on the strength of its essential oils, which diminish in time. To make sure that your spices are always fresh, buy them in quantities that you will be able to use up within two years.

Store spices in a cool, dark place~never over a stove or on an open shelf. Some cooks prefer to grind their own whole spice berries for the freshest flavor~especially nutmeg; use a quarter teaspoon less than the recipe calls for so the flavor of the freshly ground spices isn't too strong.

ALMOND MERINGUES

Makes 2½ dozen meringues

Meringue is a mixture of beaten egg whites and sugar. Here it is piped out, baked slowly in the oven, and then allowed to dry out for several hours. It may seem a bit daunting to make, but the only hard part is making sure that the mixer bowl and the beaters are scrupulously clean and that the egg whites contain no trace of yolk. Always make meringue on a day with low humidity; otherwise the baked meringue will never crisp. For a professional look, pipe the meringue onto baking sheets using a plain or star tip. You can also make meringue cookie sandwiches by spreading warm jam or melted chocolate onto the bottom of a meringue and pressing a second meringue onto the filling.

3 large egg whites, at room temperature

¼ teaspoon cream of tartar

¾ cup superfine sugar

½ teaspoon almond extract

¼ cup finely chopped almonds

1. Preheat the oven to 250°F. Line two large baking sheets with parchment paper or aluminum foil.

2. In the large bowl of an electric mixer, at medium speed, beat the egg whites until they are foamy. Beat in the cream of tartar. Increase the mixer speed to high and gradually add the sugar, 1 tablespoon at a time, beating until stiff, glossy peaks form when the beaters are lifted. Beat in the almond extract.

3. Drop the meringue by tablespoonfuls onto the lined baking sheets, placing them 1 inch apart. Sprinkle with the chopped almonds.

4. Bake for 1 hour. Turn off the oven and let the meringues dry out in the oven, with the door closed, for 4 to 5 hours, until crisp. Remove the meringues from the baking sheets and store them in an airtight container.

CLEMENTINE ALMOND CAKE

Makes 8 servings

Found in markets from November to January, clementines, members of the tangerine and mandarin orange family, are grown mainly in Spain and North Africa. A small round fruit with a shiny bright orange skin, clementines are very fragrant and juicy with an intense, sweet, orange flavor.

CAKE

1 cup all-purpose flour

1 teaspoon baking powder

⅛ teaspoon salt

1 cup granulated sugar

4 large eggs, separated

Grated zest of 2 clementines

⅔ cup strained clementine juice

1½ cups ground almonds

CREAM FROSTING AND FILLING

1½ cups heavy cream

3 tablespoons confectioners' sugar

3 tablespoons clementine or orange liqueur

¼ cup orange marmalade

Clementine zest and toasted coconut, for garnish

1. Preheat the oven to 325°F. Butter an 8-inch springform pan. Dust the pan with flour, shaking out the excess.

2. To make the cake, sift the flour, baking powder, and salt into a small bowl.

3. In the large bowl of an electric mixer, at high speed, beat the granulated sugar and egg yolks until the mixture is thick, lemon-colored, and it forms a ribbon when the beaters are lifted, about 6 minutes.

4. Reduce the mixer speed to medium and beat in the clementine zest and juice. Reduce the mixer speed to low and stir in the ground almonds. Scrape the batter into a large bowl and fold in the flour using a rubber spatula.

5. Wash the mixer bowl and beaters. Add the egg whites to the mixer bowl and beat at high speed until stiff peaks form when the beaters are lifted. With a large

Toasted almonds and tiny clementines reach high flavor notes.

rubber spatula, gently but thoroughly fold the egg whites into the batter.

6. Pour the batter into the prepared pan and place the pan on a baking sheet. Bake for 65 minutes, or until a toothpick inserted in the center comes out clean. Cool the cake in the pan on a rack for 5 minutes. Run a metal spatula around the edge of the pan to loosen the cake. Remove the pan sides and cool the cake completely on the rack. Remove the pan bottom.

7. To make the cream frosting and filling, in the chilled small bowl of the mixer, at high speed, beat the cream until soft peaks form. Gradually add the confectioners' sugar and liqueur and beat until stiff peaks form.

8. Measure ¾ cup of the cream into a small bowl and fold in the marmalade.

9. With a long, serrated knife, slice the cake in half horizontally. Place the bottom cake layer on a serving plate and spread it with the marmalade cream. Place the top cake layer over the filling.

10. Frost the top and sides of the cake with the remaining whipped cream and refrigerate the cake until you are ready to serve. Garnish the cake with the clementine zest and toasted coconut. Refrigerate any leftovers.

APPLE CAKE

Makes 8 to 10 servings

This is a dense, moist cake with a firm crumb and a brandy-flavored glaze. For the most flavorful results, use a tart cooking apple, such as Granny Smith or greening. For a more delicate flavor, choose a perfumey apple, such as Fuji or Golden Delicious. If you plan on keeping the cake for more than two days, omit the whipped cream garnish. Instead, serve softly whipped cream alongside.

SPICE CAKE

2 cups all-purpose flour

2 teaspoons baking powder

1 teaspoon ground cinnamon

1 teaspoon ground nutmeg

½ teaspoon ground ginger

½ teaspoon baking soda

¼ teaspoon salt

½ cup (1 stick) unsalted butter, at room temperature

1 cup packed light or dark brown sugar

2 large eggs, at room temperature

2 cups peeled, cored and finely shredded apple

1 cup sliced unblanched almonds

2 tablespoons brandy

1 teaspoon freshly squeezed lemon juice

1 teaspoon vanilla extract

APPLE GLAZE

¼ cup apple jelly

2 teaspoons brandy

Toasted sliced unblanched almonds and whipped cream, for garnish

1. Preheat the oven to 350°F. Generously butter an 8- by 3-inch layer-cake pan. Line the bottom of the pan with waxed paper or parchment paper cut to fit and butter the paper. Dust the pan with flour, shaking out the excess.

2. To make the spice cake, sift together the flour, baking powder, cinnamon, nutmeg, ginger, baking soda, and salt.

3. In the large bowl of an electric mixer, at medium-high speed, beat the butter until

it is creamy. Add the brown sugar and beat until the mixture is light and fluffy, scraping the side of the bowl often. Beat in the eggs until they are blended.

4. In a medium-size bowl, toss the shredded apples with the almonds, brandy, lemon juice, and vanilla. With the mixer speed at medium-low, add the apple mixture, beating just until it is well blended.

5. Reduce the mixer speed to low. Add the flour mixture all at once and mix just until blended. Spread the batter evenly in the prepared pan.

6. Bake for 45 to 50 minutes, until the top of the cake springs back when lightly touched. Let the cake cool in its pan on a rack for 10 minutes. Run a thin metal spatula around the edge of the pan to loosen the cake. Invert the cake onto the rack, peel off the paper, and let it cool completely.

7. To make the apple glaze, in a small heavy saucepan or skillet, stir the apple jelly and brandy over medium heat until the jelly is melted.

8. Place the cake on a serving plate. Spread the top of the cake with the warm glaze and sprinkle it with the toasted almonds. Pipe a border of whipped cream around the edge of the cake. Refrigerate any leftovers.

Loaded with flavor and healthy pectin, apples make desserts naturally sweet.

BURNT SUGAR COOKIES

Makes 3 dozen cookies

The crinkled tops of these cookies are reminiscent of gingersnaps, but their rich caramel flavor comes from the addition of deeply caramelized sugar syrup. To serve these cookies, arrange them in decorative rows on an old-fashioned tray along with some buttery shortbreads and chocolate-dipped crystallized ginger.

2¼ cups all-purpose flour

1½ teaspoons baking soda

1 teaspoon ground ginger

½ teaspoon ground coriander

½ teaspoon salt

¾ cup (1½ sticks) unsalted butter, at room temperature

1 cup packed light or dark brown sugar

1 teaspoon grated lemon zest

1 large egg, at room temperature

¼ cup Burnt Sugar Syrup (recipe follows)

Granulated sugar

1. Sift together the flour, baking soda, ginger, coriander, and salt.

2. In the large bowl of an electric mixer, at high speed, beat together the butter, brown sugar, and lemon zest until the mixture is light and fluffy. Reduce the mixer speed to medium. Beat in the egg and burnt sugar syrup until blended.

3. Reduce the mixer speed to low and add the dry ingredients, in two additions, mixing just until blended. Cover and refrigerate for 2 hours.

4. Preheat the oven to 350°F. Set out several baking sheets.

5. Place some granulated sugar in a pie plate. Roll spoonfuls of the cookie dough into 1-inch balls between your palms. Lightly dip half of each dough ball in water, then dip the moistened half in the sugar. Arrange the cookies, sugared side up, 2 inches apart on the baking sheets.

6. Bake for 12 to 15 minutes, until the cookies are lightly browned around the edges. Transfer the cookies to racks to cool completely. Store in an airtight container.

An old-fashioned cookie is the perfect partner for a cup of coffee.

Classic companions: a sugary almond tart held in check by coffee.

BAKEWELL TART

Makes 6 servings

PÂTE BRISÉE

2 cups all-purpose flour

2 teaspoons granulated sugar

1 teaspoon salt

¾ cup (1½ sticks) plus 2 tablespoons cold unsalted butter, cut into bits

1 large egg

1 tablespoon milk

FILLING

4 tablespoons unsalted butter, at room temperature

⅓ cup granulated sugar

1 large egg, at room temperature

1 cup pound cake crumbs (page 86))

⅔ cup ground almonds

½ teaspoon almond extract

½ cup raspberry jam

CONFECTIONERS' SUGAR GLAZE

2 tablespoons unsalted butter

1 cup confectioners' sugar

2 tablespoons heavy cream

1 teaspoon vanilla extract

1. To make the pâte brisée, in a food processor, place the flour, granulated sugar, and salt. Pulse to mix. Add the butter, pulsing several times, until the mixture forms fine crumbs.

2. In a small bowl, whisk together the egg and milk. With the processor running, gradually add the egg mixture and process until the dough pulls away from the side of the bowl and just begins to form a ball.

3. Divide the dough in half and shape each piece into a disk. Wrap one dough disk in plastic and refrigerate for at least 30 minutes, or until very firm. Wrap the second disk in heavy foil, label, and freeze for up to three months.

4. Roll the chilled dough on a floured surface into an 8-inch round. Fit the dough into a 7-inch tart pan with a removable bottom; trim the overhanging dough edge. Refrigerate the pastry shell while you make the filling.

5. Preheat the oven to 350°F.

6. For the filling, in the medium-size bowl of an electric mixer, at medium-high speed, beat the butter and granulated sugar until light and fluffy. Reduce the mixer speed to medium and beat in the egg, cake crumbs, ground almonds, and almond extract until they are blended.

7. Spread the jam evenly on the bottom of the pastry shell. Drop small mounds of the filling over the jam spreading it evenly. Place the tart on a baking sheet.

8. Bake for 30 to 40 minutes, until puffed and set in the center. Transfer to a rack.

9. While the tart is baking, make the confectioners' sugar glaze. In a medium-size saucepan, melt the butter over medium heat. Remove from the heat and stir in the confectioners' sugar, cream, and vanilla until the mixture is blended and smooth. Spread the glaze over the piping hot tart. Let the tart cool completely on the rack before serving.

Cake Crumbs

When a recipe calls for cake crumbs, choose from a mildly flavored cake such as pound or chiffon. Most of us don't bake quite as often as our mothers did, so chances are good there is not "a bit of cake going stale" to grind into crumbs. Bakeries are sometimes happy to sell cake crumbs, but lacking that, they are a good source for day-old plain cakes.

To make crumbs, you need dry cake. Place slices of cake on a baking sheet. Dry them, uncovered, in a turned-off oven or on a counter overnight. If you're in a hurry, place thick slices of cake directly on the rack of a 250°F oven for 15 to 30 minutes, watching carefully and turning the slices from time to time. Grind the dry cake in a food processor. (In a pinch, you can use challah, brioche, or packaged vanilla wafers for crumbs.)

COCONUT SHORTBREAD

Makes about 4½ dozen cookies

Crumbly, buttery, rich shortbread ~ from nursery teas on, it is a source of infinite pleasure. The dough for these cookies is very short, which makes them fragile, so carefully transfer the cut-out cookies to baking sheets with a floured spatula.

1½ cups (3 sticks) unsalted
   butter, at room temperature

1¼ cups confectioners' sugar

2⅔ cups all-purpose flour

1 cup shredded sweetened
   coconut

½ cup ground almonds

Pinch of salt

1 large egg, lightly beaten

Superfine sugar, for sprinkling

1. In the large bowl of an electric mixer, at medium-high speed, beat the butter until it is creamy. Gradually add the confectioners' sugar and beat until the mixture is light and fluffy.

2. Reduce the mixer speed to low. Add the flour in three additions, mixing until just blended after each addition. Mix in the coconut, ground almonds, and salt then stir in the egg to form a soft dough.

3. Divide the dough in half and shape each portion into a disk on a sheet of waxed paper. Wrap in plastic wrap and refrigerate for 1 hour, or until chilled.

4. Preheat the oven to 300°F. Line several baking sheets with parchment paper.

5. Roll half of the dough on a very heavily floured surface to a ¼-inch thickness. (Keep the remaining dough refrigerated.) Working quickly, cut the dough into 2-inch shapes with floured cookie cutters. (Do not use intricate shapes since the dough is soft and fragile.) Arrange the cookies 1 inch apart on the lined baking sheets. Repeat with the remaining half of the dough.

6. Bake for 15 minutes, or until the cookies are set and firm; they will not brown. Transfer the cookies to racks, sprinkle with superfine sugar, and let them cool completely. Store in an airtight container.

With cappuccino or café au lait, biscotti are the treat of the 1990's.

VANILLA HAZELNUT BISCOTTI

Makes about 5 dozen

2 large eggs

1 tablespoon Brandy

1 cup Vanilla Sugar, made with granulated sugar (page 194)

Pinch of salt

2 ¼ cups all-purpose flour

1½ teaspoons baking powder

1 cup hazelnuts, coarsely chopped

1 large egg white, lightly beaten

1. Preheat the oven to 350°F. Lightly butter and flour a large baking sheet.

2. In a medium-size bowl, beat the eggs with a fork until they are foamy. Stir in the brandy. Gradually add the vanilla sugar and salt, stirring, until the ingredients are well blended. Set the mixture aside.

3. Sift the flour and baking powder into a large bowl. Make a well in the center of the dry ingredients. Add the egg mixture, stirring with a fork, until the flour is evenly moistened and the mixture is crumbly.

4. Turn the flour mixture out onto a lightly floured work surface. Gently knead the dough, gradually incorporating the hazelnuts. When the dough becomes smooth, divide it in half.

5. Shape each portion of dough into a log about 16 inches long and 1 inch in diameter. Arrange the logs on the prepared baking sheet about 2 inches apart. Brush the logs with the beaten egg white.

6. Bake the logs for 25 to 30 minutes, until they are golden brown. Cool them on the baking sheet, set on a rack, for 15 minutes. Meanwhile, reduce the oven temperature to 300°F.

7. Using a serrated knife, cut the logs into diagonal slices about ½ inch thick. Stand the slices upright on the baking sheet.

8. Bake the slices for 20 minutes, or until the biscotti are dry and lightly golden. Let them cool, still on the baking sheet, set on the rack.

Tea Cakes with Marmalade Cream Filling

(recipe on page 106)

T E A

As the day begins to wind down, the magical hour of four draws near ~ time for afternoon tea, a gracious and elegant interlude when the mundane and the routine make way for fine bone china, cut crystal, and heirloom lace; when friends exchange news of the day and lighthearted conversation fills the air. What Queen Victoria perfected more than a century ago becomes for each of us a personal moment of luxurious respite from the cares and chaos of modern life. The aroma of freshly brewed jasmine tea wafts through the air as lemon, cream, and sugar are set out and silver trays are filled with an indulgent array of freshly baked delights. In this chapter are the quintessential sweets to accompany this most delightful of rituals, from light cherry-filled scones to refreshing lemon tarts to extraordinary nut-studded candied fruitcakes.

ALMOND FRUITCAKE

Makes 12 to 16 servings

Fruitcakes have been a family holiday tradition for generations, with recipes passed down from mother to daughter. They have fallen from grace in recent times, but this recipe, crumbly with ground almonds and rich with candied citrus peel, crystallized ginger, and raisins, will undoubtedly restore them to favor.

1 cup all-purpose flour

Pinch of salt

2¼ cups mixed golden and dark raisins (12 ounces)

½ cup chopped mixed candied orange and lemon peel (3 ounces)

¼ cup finely chopped crystallized ginger (1 ounce)

1 cup (2 sticks) unsalted butter, at room temperature

1 cup plus 2 tablespoons sugar

4 large eggs, at room temperature

2¼ cups ground almonds (8 ounces)

Grated zest of 1 medium-size orange

Whole almonds, for garnish (optional)

1. Preheat the oven to 300°F. Butter an 8- by 3-inch layer-cake pan. Line the pan bottom and side with buttered waxed paper, allowing the waxed paper to extend about ½ inch above the rim of the pan.

2. In a small bowl, stir together the flour and salt. In a medium-size bowl, stir together the raisins, candied peel, and crystallized ginger. Add ¼ cup of the flour mixture and toss to coat.

3. In the large bowl of an electric mixer, at medium-high speed, beat the butter until it is creamy. Gradually add the sugar and beat until the mixture is light and fluffy, scraping down the side of the bowl once or twice.

4. Beat in the eggs, one at a time, alternately with half of the ground almonds (1 cup plus 2 tablespoons), beating well after each addition.

Don't wait for a holiday: a golden fruitcake is wonderful any time.

5. Gradually stir in the remaining ground almonds and the flour mixture. Lastly, fold in the raisin and candied peel mixture and the freshly grated orange zest.

6. Pour the batter into the prepared pan and smooth the top. If desired, decorate the top with whole almonds.

7. Bake for 1¾ to 2 hours, until a toothpick inserted in the center comes out clean. Let the cake cool in the pan on a rack for 30 minutes. Gently loosen the waxed paper from the side of the pan with a small knife. Turn the cake out of the pan onto the rack and peel off the paper. Let the cake cool completely.

8. Wrap the cooled cake in brandy-soaked cheesecloth and then in foil. Refrigerate the cake at least overnight before cutting into thin slices to serve.

DORSET APPLE CAKE

Makes 12 servings

Autumn, the time of year when the perfume of apples is in the air, is when you'll want to bake this richly textured loaf cake. Serve this with Saga blue or slices of sharp Cheddar cheese ~ their flavor marries well with the tart apple in the cake.

1¾ cups all-purpose flour

½ cup sugar

1 tablespoon baking powder

½ cup (1 stick) cold unsalted butter, cut into bits

1 large tart apple, peeled, cored and finely chopped (about 1¼ cups)

½ cup milk

1 large egg

1. Preheat the oven to 350°F. Butter an 8½- by 4½- by 2¾-inch glass loaf pan. Line the bottom of the pan with waxed paper cut to fit and butter the paper. Dust the pan with flour, shaking out the excess.

2. Sift the flour, sugar, and baking powder into a large bowl. With a pastry blender or two knives, cut in the butter until the mixture forms a fine meal. Add the apple and toss to mix.

3. In a small bowl, whisk together the milk and egg. Stir this into the apple and flour mixture until blended. (The batter will be stiff.) With a spatula, spread the batter evenly in the prepared pan.

4. Bake for 45 to 50 minutes, until a toothpick inserted in the center comes out clean. Let the cake cool in the pan on a rack for 10 minutes. Run a thin metal spatula around the edges to loosen the cake and invert it onto the rack. Peel off the paper and let the cake cool completely. Let the cake age for at least one day before you serve it for the very best flavor.

ROYAL CRESCENT SCONES

Makes 10 to 12 scones

This recipe comes from the Royal Crescent Hotel in the Georgian city of Bath, England. All scones are at their best when served fresh from the oven, and these are no exception. They should be enjoyed for afternoon tea with a bowl of authentic clotted cream and a jar of homemade strawberry jam.

3⅔ cups all-purpose flour

6 tablespoons cold unsalted butter, cut into bits

½ cup superfine sugar

2 teaspoons baking powder

¼ teaspoon salt

3 tablespoons golden raisins (optional)

1 to 1¼ cups milk, plus additional for brushing the scones

1. Preheat the oven to 400°F. Lightly butter a baking sheet.

2. Put the flour into a large bowl. With a pastry blender or two knives, cut the butter into the flour until the mixture forms a coarse meal. Add the sugar, the baking powder, salt, and raisins (if you are using them), and toss to mix.

3. Gradually add enough of the milk to form a soft dough. Turn the dough out onto a floured surface and knead it gently with your fingertips several times to form a smooth dough.

4. Roll the dough on the floured surface to a 1¼-inch thickness. Cut out scones with a floured 2-inch biscuit cutter. Reroll the dough scraps once and cut out additional scones. Arrange the scones 2 inches apart on the baking sheet and lightly brush the tops of the scones with milk.

5. Bake for 20 minutes, or until golden brown. Serve while hot and fresh.

A mainstay of baking, gingerbread traces its origins to antiquity.

GINGERBREAD
WITH LEMON VERBENA MOUSSE

Makes 8 to 10 servings

Martha Washington, our first First Lady, gave us this "recipt." Here it's has been updated slightly, although in keeping with tradition, the gingerbread doesn't contain eggs. The cake is a bit denser than most, but it's spiced just right, and the gingerbread is a delicious foil for the creamy lemon mousse filling. Do search out lavender honey if you can, but lacking that, use wildflower honey instead.

GINGERBREAD

2 cups sifted all-purpose flour

1 teaspoon baking soda

1 teaspoon ground ginger

¼ teaspoon ground cinnamon

Pinch of ground cloves

Pinch of ground nutmeg

1 cup molasses

5 tablespoons unsalted butter, at room temperature

1 tablespoon honey, preferably lavender

1 tablespoon pumpkin puree or applesauce

½ cup boiling water

LEMON VERBENA MOUSSE

½ cup plus 1½ tablespoons granulated sugar

½ cup freshly squeezed lemon juice

4 large egg yolks

1 tablespoon honey, preferably lavender

1 sprig lemon verbena, lemon balm, or mint

½ cup heavy cream

BUTTERCREAM FROSTING

½ cup (1 stick) unsalted butter, at room temperature

1½ cups confectioners' sugar, plus additional for rolling the marzipan

1 teaspoon vanilla extract

One 7- to 8-ounce package marzipan

Fresh raspberries, blackberries, blueberries, and sliced figs, or other seasonal fruit, for garnish

1. Preheat the oven to 375°F. Butter two 8-inch layer-cake pans. Line the pan bottoms with waxed paper cut to fit and butter the paper. Dust the pans with flour, shaking out the excess.

2. To make the gingerbread, in the large bowl of an electric mixer, at low speed, stir the flour, baking soda, ginger, cinnamon, cloves, and nutmeg until blended.

3. Add the molasses, butter, honey, and pumpkin puree to the flour mixture. Increase the mixer speed to medium and beat the batter until it is smooth. Beat in the boiling water. Pour the batter into the prepared pans.

4. Bake for 20 to 25 minutes, until the top springs back when lightly touched and a toothpick inserted in the center comes out clean. (The cakes will not fill the pans.) Let the cakes cool in their pans on racks for 10 minutes. Run a thin metal spatula around the edge of the pans to loosen the cakes and turn them out onto the racks. Peel off the paper and let them cool completely.

5. Meanwhile, make the lemon verbena mousse. In a heavy medium-size non-reactive saucepan, whisk together ½ cup plus 1 tablespoon of the granulated sugar, the lemon juice, egg yolks, and honey until they are blended. Add the sprig of lemon verbena. Cook over medium heat, whisking constantly, until the mixture is extremely thick and almost boiling, about 30 minutes.

6. Remove the herb sprig. Pour the warm custard into a medium-size bowl. Press plastic wrap directly onto the surface and refrigerate until cool.

7. In the chilled small bowl of the mixer, at high speed, beat the cream and the remaining ½ tablespoon granulated sugar until stiff peaks form. With a rubber spatula, gradually fold the cream into the cooled custard. Cover and refrigerate while making the buttercream frosting.

8. In the medium-size bowl of the mixer, at medium-high speed, beat the butter until it is creamy. Sift in the confectioners' sugar, in three additions, beating until smooth. Beat in the vanilla.

9. To assemble, place one cake on a serving plate. Reserve ½ cup of the lemon verbena mousse and spread the remaining mousse on the cake layer.

10. Top with the second cake layer. Spread the top only with the buttercream frosting. Using a small metal spatula, spread a thin layer of the reserved mousse around the side of the cake. With a measuring tape, measure the cir-

cumference and the height of the cake. Refrigerate the cake to keep it firm.

11. To make the marzipan edging, roll out the marzipan on a surface dusted with confectioners' sugar to a strip the same length as the circumference of the cake and the same width as the height of the cake. Using a ruler and a knife, trim the edges of the marzipan strip even.

12. For easier handling, cut the marzipan strip in half crosswise. Carefully wrap the marzipan strips around the side of the cake. Garnish the top of the cake with some of the fruit and refrigerate until 30 minutes before you are ready to serve.

13. To serve, cut the cake into wedges, place on dessert plates, and spoon the remaining fruit alongside the cake.

Lush fresh flowers make a spectacular garnish for cakes and cupcakes, but pick your flowers wisely. The flowers should be free of pesticides and be edible (even if they are not eaten). Pick flowers from your garden, or look for them at gourmet shops. They will keep for up to one week if well wrapped and stored in the refrigerator. Here are especially pretty flowers to choose from: Chrysanthemums • Daisies • Geraniums • Johnny Jump Ups • Lavender • Lilacs • Marigolds • Nasturtiums • Pansies • Roses • Violets • Violas

WHIDBEY ISLAND LOGANBERRY LIQUEUR CAKE

Makes 2 dozen small squares

The special liqueur for this recipe is produced on Whidbey Island, located off the coast of Washington State in Puget Sound. Its raspberry-like flavor is the perfect complement to the very chocolate cake layers and the rich whipped cream filling in this truly decadent dessert.

LIQUEUR CAKE

1¾ cups all-purpose flour

1 teaspoon baking soda

¾ teaspoon salt

3 tablespoons Whidbey Island Loganberry Liqueur or raspberry liqueur

½ cup (1 stick) unsalted butter, at room temperature

1¾ cups sugar

Four 1-ounce squares unsweetened chocolate, melted and cooled

4 large eggs, at room temperature

¾ cup milk

FILLING

Four and one half 1-ounce squares semisweet chocolate, coarsely chopped

One 1-ounce square unsweetened chocolate, coarsely chopped

1 cup plus 3 tablespoons heavy cream

3 tablespoons seedless raspberry jam

1 tablespoon Whidbey Island Loganberry Liqueur or raspberry liqueur

1. Preheat the oven to 300°F. Butter a 13- by 9-inch baking pan. Dust the pan with flour, shaking out the excess.

2. To make the liqueur cake, sift together the flour, baking soda, and salt.

3. Put the liqueur into a 1-cup glass measure. Add enough water to equal ½ cup.

4. In the large bowl of an electric mixer, at medium speed, beat the butter and sugar until they are light and fluffy. Gradually pour in the melted chocolate,

Gorgeous and glamourous, a cake that inspires an endless tea time.

beating until blended, scraping down the side of the bowl once or twice.

5. Add the eggs, one at a time, beating well after each addition. Add the flour in three additions, alternately with the milk and the diluted liqueur, beating after each addition just until smooth, and scraping down the side of the bowl often. Spread the batter evenly in the prepared pan.

6. Bake for 50 minutes, or until a toothpick inserted in the center comes out clean. Let the cake cool in the pan on a rack for 10 minutes. Run a metal spatula round the edge of the pan to loosen the cake and invert it onto the rack. Let the cake cool completely.

7. Meanwhile, make the filling. In the top of a double boiler over barely simmering water, melt the semisweet chocolate, unsweetened chocolate, and 3 tablespoons of the cream, stirring frequently, until smooth. Pour the chocolate into a medium-size bowl and let it cool to room temperature, stirring often.

8. Stir the jam to soften it, then gradually stir it into the cooled chocolate mixture.

9. In the chilled small bowl of the mixer, at high speed, beat the remaining 1 cup of cream until soft peaks form. Add the liqueur and beat until stiff peaks form. Stir a few spoonfuls of the whipped cream into the chocolate mixture, then fold in the remaining cream.

10. To assemble, with a long serrated knife, cut the cake in half horizontally. Place the bottom layer on a serving plate and spread with the filling. Top with the remaining cake layer and refrigerate until you are ready to serve.

11. To serve, cut the cake into small squares and dust with confectioners' sugar.

DUNDEE CAKE

Makes 12 to 16 servings

Dundee cake originated in the early nineteenth century in the town of Dundee in Scotland. A generous quantity of raisins, currants, and candied fruit peel, along with the classic topping of almonds, sets this cake apart from other fruitcakes. Age becomes it, so keep it for at least one day, although several weeks would be even better. While it is aging, brush it a few times with brandy or Scotch whisky, which will mellow the flavor and improve the crumb.

1¾ cups all-purpose flour

1 teaspoon baking powder

½ teaspoon ground cinnamon

⅛ teaspoon ground nutmeg

⅛ teaspoon salt

1⅓ cups currants

1 cup chopped dark raisins

¾ cup chopped golden raisins

⅓ cup chopped mixed candied orange and lemon peel (2 ounces)

¾ cup (1½ sticks) unsalted butter, at room temperature

¾ cup plus 2 tablespoons superfine sugar

3 large eggs, well beaten

2 tablespoons brandy or milk

Grated zest of 1 medium-size lemon

½ cup chopped blanched almonds

1. Preheat the oven to 350°F. Butter a 7½- by 2½-inch springform pan. Line the bottom of the pan with waxed paper cut to fit and butter the paper. Dust the pan with flour, shaking out the excess.

2. Sift the flour, baking powder, cinnamon, nutmeg, and salt into a medium-size bowl.

3. In another medium-size bowl, combine the currants, dark and golden raisins, and the candied peel. Add ¼ cup of the flour mixture and toss to coat the fruit.

4. In the large bowl of an electric mixer, at medium speed, beat the butter until it is creamy. Gradually add the sugar and beat until light and fluffy. Add the eggs, one-third at a time, beating well after each addition. (Add a little of the flour mixture if the batter looks curdled.) Beat in the brandy or milk.

5. Reduce the mixer speed to low and gradually add the flour mixture, beating until just blended. Add the raisin mixture, lemon zest, and ¼ cup of the almonds.

6. Pour the batter into the prepared pan and spread it evenly. Sprinkle the surface with the remaining ¼ cup almonds.

7. Bake for 45 minutes. Reduce the oven temperature to 300°F. Bake 1 to 1¼ hours longer, until a toothpick inserted in the center comes out clean.

8. Let the cake cool in the pan on a rack for 10 minutes. Run a spatula around the edge of the pan to loosen the cake and remove the pan side. Let the cake cool completely on the rack, then remove the pan bottom and peel off the paper.

9. Wrap the cake in brandy-soaked cheesecloth and overwrap in foil.

Plump raisins and spicy-sweet currants impart flavor, moisture, and old-fashioned appeal to cookies, cakes, and pies.

In their dried form, Corinth grapes become Zante currants, while Thompson seedless green grapes become the dark raisins we are all so familiar with. Golden raisins, dried indoors, are treated to prevent them from darkening. This process renders them so moist they need not be plumped before use.

A handful of raisins can be added to most recipes by lightly coating them in some of the flour mixture before stirring them into the batter. This will prevent them from sinking. For truly irresistible raisins, plump them in orange juice, brandy, rum, or your favorite liqueur.

CHERRY-FILLED SCONES

Makes 32 scones

These orange-scented scones are best served warm and bubbling right from the oven with a good strong cup of tea, such as Russian caravan or orange pekoe. The recipe calls for only a little of the delicious cherry filling, so save the remainder for spooning onto thick slices of toasted brioche for a breakfast treat.

SCONES

2 cups all-purpose flour

¼ cup sugar

1 tablespoon plus 1 teaspoon baking powder

1 tablespoon grated orange zest

Pinch of salt

1 cup heavy cream

¼ cup freshly squeezed orange juice

2 tablespoons cooled Cherry Filling (recipe follows), or cherry preserves

1. Preheat the oven to 350°F. Butter two baking sheets.
2. In a large bowl, stir together the flour, sugar, baking powder, orange zest, and salt until they are well blended.
3. Gradually add the cream and orange juice, stirring with a fork to form a soft dough which pulls away from the side of the bowl.
4. Turn the dough out onto a floured surface and gently knead ten times with your fingertips. Divide the dough in half. Roll each half of the dough into a 9-inch round, about ¼ inch thick.
5. Cut out scones using a floured 3-inch biscuit cutter. Spoon ½ teaspoon of the cherry filling on one half of each round. Fold the other half of the dough over the filling and pinch the edges together to seal. Arrange the scones 2 inches apart on the prepared baking sheets.
6. Bake for 15 minutes, or until nicely browned. Serve hot.

Not-too-sweet scones with a deep, buttery flavor bake up tender.

CHERRY FILLING

¼ cup cornstarch

2 tablespoons sugar

1 tablespoon freshly squeezed
lemon juice

1½ cups pitted fresh sour
cherries or half a 16-ounce
package frozen pitted sour
cherries, thawed, with juice

1. In a heavy medium-size nonreactive saucepan, stir together the cornstarch and sugar. Whisk in ½ cup of cold water until smooth. Place over medium heat and cook, whisking constantly, until the mixture starts to thicken. Remove the saucepan from the heat.

2. Add the cherries and stir to mix well. Return to medium heat and cook, stirring constantly, until the juices thicken and boil. Remove from the heat and stir in the lemon juice. (The filling will be very thick.)

3. Let the cherry filling come to room temperature before using.

TEA CAKES WITH MARMALADE CREAM FILLING

(PHOTOGRAPH ON PAGE 90)

Makes 28 to 30 tea cakes

These spectacular-looking individual cakes resemble beautiful butterfly wings when assembled. Though they're whimsical in appearance, the combination of coffee, chocolate, and orange gives them a decidedly sophisticated air.

TEA CAKES

- 2 cups self-rising flour
- 1½ cups granulated sugar
- 1 teaspoon baking powder
- 1 cup milk
- 3 large eggs, at room temperature
- ½ cup (1 stick) unsalted butter, at room temperature
- 2 teaspoons vanilla extract
- Two 1-ounce squares semisweet chocolate, melted and cooled
- 2 tablespoons cold strong coffee
- ¼ cup orange marmalade

MARMALADE CREAM FILLING

- ½ cup granulated sugar
- ¼ cup freshly squeezed lemon juice
- 2 cups heavy cream
- 1 teaspoon vanilla extract
- ½ cup orange marmalade

Confectioners' sugar and candied cherries, cut into pieces, for garnish

1. Preheat the oven to 375°F. Butter and flour 28 to 30 muffin cups, or line them with paper liners.
2. To make the tea cakes, in the large bowl of an electric mixer, stir together the flour, granulated sugar, and baking powder until blended.
3. Add the milk, eggs, butter, and vanilla and beat at low speed for 1 minute to

blend, scraping the side of the bowl often. Increase the mixer speed to high and beat for 3 minutes, or until the batter is smooth.

4. Transfer half the batter to another bowl. With the mixer at medium speed, beat the chocolate and coffee into the batter until they are blended. Stir the marmalade into the other half of the batter.

5. Spoon the marmalade batter into 14 or 15 of the prepared muffin cups, filling them half full. Spoon the chocolate batter into the remaining muffin cups, filling the cups half full.

6. Bake for 18 to 20 minutes, until a toothpick inserted in the center comes out clean. Let the tea cakes cool in the pans on racks for 10 minutes, then turn them out of the pans onto the racks to cool completely.

7. While the tea cakes cool, make the marmalade cream filling. In a small saucepan, bring the granulated sugar and ¼ cup of water to a rolling boil, stirring constantly. Stir in the lemon juice, remove from the heat, and refrigerate until cold.

8. In the chilled medium-size bowl of the mixer, gradually whisk the chilled lemon syrup into the cream. Stir in the vanilla. Beat at medium-high speed until stiff peaks form. With a rubber spatula, fold in the orange marmalade.

9. To fill the tea cakes, gently cut a small circle in the top of each tea cake with a small serrated knife, leaving a ⅜-inch wide rim and cutting only halfway down. Cut this circular piece in half. Using the tip of the knife, gently lift out each semicircle of cake from the center, being careful to keep the pieces intact.

10. Mound about 2 tablespoons of the marmalade cream filling into the center of each tea cake. Replace the cake tops. Add a small spoonful of filling between the pieces of cake tops.

11. Dust the tea cakes with confectioners' sugar and garnish with cherry pieces. Refrigerate any leftovers.

LEMON SQUARES

Makes 2 dozen squares

Luscious confections with just the right combination of sweet and tart, these cakes are a wonderful treat, especially when served with lemon-scented tea. The recipe is courtesy of Charlotte Béro, mother of Craig Béro, who is proprietor of the Anglers and Writers restaurant in New York City. Craig couldn't find anyone who could bake as well as his mother, so Charlotte became his pastry chef.

BUTTER CRUST

1¾ cups all-purpose flour

¾ cup (1½ sticks) plus 2 tablespoons cold unsalted butter, cut into bits

¼ cup confectioners' sugar

LEMON FILLING

1½ cups granulated sugar

3 large eggs

2 tablespoons grated lemon zest

½ cup freshly squeezed lemon juice

⅓ cup all-purpose flour

½ teaspoon baking powder

Confectioners' sugar, for garnish

1. Preheat the oven to 350°F. Set out a 13- by 9-inch baking pan.
2. To make the butter crust, in the large bowl of an electric mixer, at low speed, beat the flour, butter, and confectioners' sugar for 1 minute.
3. Increase the mixer speed to medium and beat for 4 minutes, until the mixture forms coarse crumbs, scraping the side of the bowl often. Press the dough into the bottom of the pan.
4. Bake for 15 minutes, or until the crust is firm but not brown. Let the crust cool in the pan on a rack while making the lemon filling.
5. To make the lemon filling, in the medium-size bowl of the mixer, at low speed, beat together the granulated sugar, eggs, the lemon zest and juice, the flour, and baking powder until just blended. Pour over the baked crust.

Mom's cooking at its best: the classic, nostalgic lemon squares.

6. Bake for 25 minutes, or until the filling is firm when lightly touched in the center. Allow the lemon squares to cool completely in the pan on a rack.

7. Sprinkle with a dusting of confectioners' sugar and cut into squares to serve. Refrigerate any leftovers.

An Old~Fashioned Baker

From New York City to the small farming community of Algoma, Wisconsin may seem far to go to find the perfect pastry chef. But for Craig Béro, proprietor of New York's popular restaurant Anglers & Writers, it was a distance marked by memories, not miles. That's because the chef in question was his mother, Charlotte Béro.

When it came time to open his new restaurant, Craig was haunted by recollections of his mother's baked goods. Sour cherry pies, brimming with just-harvested fruits from family orchards, shortbread hearts, and tangy lemon bars were as much a part of Craig's childhood as fresh air and sunshine. Devoted to the goal of serving only the highest quality at Anglers & Writers, Craig realized the only pastry chef who could duplicate the glories of Mom's baking was Mom herself. So Charlotte Béro, in the tradition of great mothers, answered her son's plea for help. Packing up a large sack of

The charm of the farm, beautifully presented.

apples and a recipe book handwritten by her own mother, Charlotte set about to show the city folks how it's done on the farm. Just as Craig envisioned, customers fell so deeply in love with his mother's pies, cakes, and other desserts that Charlotte has hardly had time to pause between batches of cookies, or to teach at the New York City cooking schools where she is always in demand.

Located in Manhattan's historic Greenwich Village, Anglers & Writers — a name that gives tribute to Craig's two passions—fits right into New York City's most artistic neighborhood. Fresh flowers, pretty lace doilies, and exquisite china will invite the visitor to contemplate the array of desserts in a leisurely manner. Whether one chooses the scones bursting with cherries, apricots, apples, and raisins, or a piece the juicy strawberry rhubarb pie to accompany a steaming cup of tea or coffee, all will be sure to recognize the unmistakable difference that old-fashioned methods and farm-fresh ingredients can make.

TEA AND BUTTON TARTS

Makes 2 dozen tarts

Betty Jean Dyvig, who makes her living creating small fantasies such as exquisite hand-painted teapots and doll-size furniture, is responsible for these adorable tarts, which look just like big buttons. When she was a little girl, Betty Jean loved having a tiny cake all to herself at teatime; now that she's grown up, she bakes these for the pleasure of her friends' children.

½ cup (1 stick) unsalted butter, at room temperature

⅓ cup sugar

1⅔ cups all-purpose flour

1 large egg, at room temperature

1 teaspoon cream or milk

¾ cup strawberry jam

1. In a medium-size bowl, beat the butter and sugar with a wooden spoon until creamy. Add the flour, egg, and cream and stir until a dough forms.

2. Cut the dough in half and shape each half into a disk. Wrap each in plastic and refrigerate for 2 hours, or until the dough is well chilled.

3. Preheat the oven to 350°F. Set out twelve 1½-inch tartlet molds that are ¾-inch deep (or use 1¾-inch miniature muffin tins).

4. Keeping half the dough refrigerated, roll one half on a lightly floured surface to ⅛-inch thickness. Using a lightly floured biscuit cutter, cut the dough into 12 rounds large enough to fit the tartlet molds or muffin tins. With a floured thumb, press the dough into the molds, trimming the excess dough from the rims. Place the molds on a baking sheet. Gather the dough scraps into a ball, wrap in plastic, and set them aside.

5. Bake for 12 to 15 minutes, until the shells are lightly browned. Allow the shells to cool completely in the pans on a rack. When cooled, remove the pastry shells from the molds or the muffin tin. Leave the oven turned on.

6. Using the dough scraps, cut out 12 rounds of dough, ½ inch smaller than the

Like Linzer Tarts with imagination, jam-filled cookie sandwiches.

tops of the tart shells. Using a skewer, make four holes in the center of each dough round to resemble a button.

7. Roll the remaining dough scraps into 12 thin ropes about ¼ inch in diameter. Use the ropes to form a ring of dough around the outside of each dough "button," creating a raised "rim" on the outer edge of the buttons. Pinch the ends of the ropes together to seal. The buttons should now be about the same diameter as the tops of the tarts.

8. Arrange the buttons 2 inches apart on a lightly buttered baking sheet. Bake for 10 minutes, or until the centers are lightly browned. (Watch carefully as the centers overbrown quickly.) Transfer to a rack to cool completely.

9. Repeat making tart shells and buttons with the remaining refrigerated dough.

10. To assemble, fill each tart shell to the top with some strawberry jam and place a pastry button on top of each tart.

RASPBERRY PECAN SCONES

Makes 15 to 18 scones

The double fruit flavor of both raspberry syrup and raspberry preserves gives these scones their uniqueness. A piped swirl of softened cream cheese lends a rich creaminess that makes them simply divine at teatime.

2 cups all-purpose flour

1 tablespoon baking powder

¼ teaspoon baking soda

¼ teaspoon salt

4 tablespoons cold unsalted butter, cut into bits

½ cup ground pecans

⅓ cup heavy cream

¼ cup raspberry syrup

1 large egg, at room temperature

Softened unsalted butter

½ cup raspberry preserves

One 3-ounce package cream cheese, at room temperature

1 teaspoon milk

1. Preheat the oven to 400°F. Butter a baking sheet.

2. In a medium-size bowl, mix the flour, baking powder, baking soda, and salt.

3. With a pastry blender or two knives, cut in the butter until the mixture forms a coarse meal. Stir in the pecans and make a well in the center.

4. In a small bowl, whisk together the cream, raspberry syrup, and egg until they are blended. Pour the mixture into the well and stir quickly with a fork just until the dough begins to form a ball.

5. Turn the dough onto a floured surface and lightly knead with your fingertips for about 30 seconds. Gently pat the dough into a ½-inch thick circle. Cut out the scones with a floured 2-inch biscuit cutter. Arrange the scones about 1 inch apart on the prepared baking sheet.

6. Bake the scones for 10 to 12 minutes, until they are golden brown. Transfer the scones to a rack and let stand until warm.

7. To serve, split the scones in half horizontally. Lightly butter the insides and

spread each scone with about 1 teaspoon of the raspberry preserves. Gently sandwich the scone halves together.

8. In a small bowl, beat the cream cheese and milk until smooth. Put the cream cheese mixture into a small pastry bag fitted with a small star or plain tip and pipe a lacy pattern on the top of each scone.

Scones, so essential to teatime, hail from Scotland. Scones may be sweet or savory, rich with butter and sugar, or plain and simple. The dough may be patted into a round and cut into wedges, or rolled and stamped out with a floured biscuit cutter.

Nowadays, scones are usually baked in the oven, but originally, they were baked on a old-fashioned stove-top griddle.

There is only one rule when making scones—always use a light hand when stirring, kneading, and shaping.

The classic way to enjoy a scone is to break off a piece and spread it with homemade jam and a spoonful of thick clotted cream. Absolutely delicious.

VICTORIA SPONGE CAKE

Makes 8 servings

Also known as Victoria Sandwich, this cake was named after one of England's most popular queens. It is a traditional British teatime favorite, served sliced and filled with good homemade strawberry or raspberry jam. With a pitcher of iced lapsang souchong or minted tea, it's delightfully refreshing.

SPONGE CAKE

2 cups cake flour

2 teaspoons baking powder

¼ teaspoon salt

1 cup granulated sugar

Zest of half a medium-size lemon, removed with a vegetable peeler and coarsely chopped

1 cup (2 sticks) unsalted butter, at room temperature

4 large eggs, at room temperature

2 tablespoons warm milk

½ teaspoon vanilla extract

1 cup strawberry jam, preferably homemade

2 cups heavy cream, whipped

Pesticide-free edible flowers, for garnish

1. Preheat the oven to 350°F. Lightly butter two 8- by 1½-inch layer-cake pans. Dust the pans with flour, shaking out the excess.

2. To make the sponge cake, sift together the flour, baking powder, and salt twice.

3. In a food processor, process the sugar and lemon zest until the zest is finely chopped, about 1 minute. Pour the sugar into the large bowl of an electric mixer. Add the butter and beat at medium speed about 3 minutes, until light.

4. In a 2-cup glass measure, whisk together the eggs, milk, and vanilla. Add to the butter mixture, about 2 tablespoons at a time, beating well after each addition, and adding 1 tablespoon of the flour mixture during the last three additions.

A veil of whipped cream shelters a delicious, plain sponge cake.

5. Gradually add the remaining flour mixture, beating until the batter is smooth and shiny. Pour the batter into the prepared pans and smooth the tops.

6. Bake for 25 to 30 minutes, until the tops are golden brown and spring back when lightly touched in the center. Let the cakes cool in their pans on racks for 10 minutes. Run a thin metal spatula around the edge of the pans to loosen the cakes and turn the cakes out onto the racks to cool completely.

7. To assemble, place one cake layer on a serving plate. Spread with the jam and 2 cups of the whipped cream, leaving a 1-inch border around the edge. Top with the second cake layer, placing it bottom side up. Spread the remaining 2 cups whipped cream over the top of the cake.

8. Refrigerate the cake. Just before serving, arrange flowers in the center of the cake. For easy serving, dip a slicing knife in cold water, shake off the excess, and cut the cake into wedges, dipping the knife into water as each slice is cut.

LEMON THYME POPPIES

Makes 40 tea cakes

If you need a reason to grow lemon thyme, these sweet little tea cakes are it. The herb, which will happily grow in a flowerpot placed on a sunny windowsill, gracefully complements all manner of savory foods as well as cakes and desserts.

TEA CAKE BATTER

1¼ cups all-purpose flour

½ teaspoon baking powder

½ teaspoon baking soda

¼ teaspoon salt

½ cup (1 stick) unsalted butter, at room temperature

½ cup granulated sugar

2 large eggs, at room temperature

½ cup lemon yogurt

2 teaspoons grated lemon zest

1 teaspoon fresh lemon thyme leaves

1 teaspoon poppy seeds

½ teaspoon vanilla extract

ORANGE GLAZE

2 cups confectioners' sugar

⅓ cup freshly squeezed orange juice

1 tablespoon unsalted butter, melted

1. Arrange one rack in the top third of the oven and preheat the oven to 375°F. Butter and flour 30 miniature (1¾-inch) muffin cups or line them with paper or foil liners.

2. To make the tea cake batter, in a small bowl, stir together the flour, baking powder, baking soda, and salt.

3. In the large bowl of an electric mixer, at medium-high speed, beat the butter until it is creamy. Gradually add the granulated sugar, beating until light and

fluffy. Add the eggs, one at a time, beating well after each addition.

4. Reduce the mixer speed to low. Add the flour mixture in three additions, alternately with the yogurt, beating just until blended after each addition, and beginning and ending with the flour.

5. Stir in the lemon zest, lemon thyme, poppy seeds, and vanilla. Spoon into the prepared muffin cups, filling them three-quarters full.

6. Bake the tea cakes in the top third of the oven for 12 to 15 minutes, until a toothpick inserted in the center comes out clean. Place the tea cakes on racks.

7. Make the orange glaze. Sift the confectioners' sugar into a medium-size bowl. Gradually whisk in the orange juice and the melted butter, whisking the mixture until the glaze is nice and smooth.

8. Remove the hot tea cakes from the pans, and if necessary, peel off the paper liners. Dip each tea cake in the glaze, turning to coat them completely. Cool the tea cakes on racks set over waxed paper.

Brewing a Proper Pot of Tea

Isabella Beeton, who in her *Book of Household Management*, penned the rigid rules for social etiquette in Victorian and Edwardian England, also offered sage advice for brewing tea.

"There is very little art in making good tea; if the water is boiling, and there is no sparing of the fragrant leaf, the beverage will almost invariably be good. The old-fashioned plan of allowing a teaspoonful to each person, and one over, is still practised. Warm the teapot with boiling water . . . for two or three minutes . . . then pour it away. Put in the tea, pour in from ½ to ¾ pint of boiling water, close the lid, and let it stand for the tea to draw from 5 to 10 minutes; then fill up the pot with water. The tea will be quite spoiled unless made with water that is actually boiling, as the leaves will not open, and the flavor not be extracted from them."

TEAROOM PEACHES

Makes 30 to 32 cookiess

A trompe l'oeil dessert, these peaches aren't peaches at all, but cookies filled with a mixture of apricot jam, melted chocolate, and ground hazelnuts.

COLORED SUGARS

1 cup sugar

Red and yellow liquid food coloring

COOKIES

3¾ cups all-purpose flour

1 cup sugar

¾ teaspoon baking powder

¾ cup (1½ sticks) unsalted butter, at room temperature

½ cup milk

2 large eggs, at room temperature

¾ teaspoon vanilla extract

FILLING

⅔ cup apricot jam

⅓ cup skinned and finely ground hazelnuts

¼ cup semisweet chocolate chips, melted and cooled

2 teaspoons orange juice

Cinnamon sticks and pesticide-free edible leaves, for garnish (optional)

1. Preheat the oven to 400°F. Set out a 10-inch and a 7-inch pie plate.
2. To make the colored sugars, in the 10-inch pie plate, put ⅔ cup of the sugar and 2 drops each of red and yellow food coloring. Rub the color evenly into the sugar with the back of a spoon.

3. In the 7-inch pie plate, put the remaining ⅓ cup sugar and 2 drops of red food coloring. Rub the color evenly into the sugar with the back of a spoon.

4. Heat the pans of sugar in the oven for 5 to 15 minutes, until the sugar is dry, stirring occasionally. Remove from the oven and place on racks to cool. Reduce the oven temperature to 325°F.

5. To make the cookies, in the large bowl of an electric mixer, at low speed, mix together 2 cups of the flour, the sugar, and baking powder until blended.

6. Add the butter, milk, eggs, and vanilla and beat for 30 seconds, scraping the side of the bowl frequently with a rubber spatula. Then increase the mixer speed to medium and beat for 1 minute.

7. With the mixer at low speed, or by hand, stir in the remaining 1¾ cups flour to make a soft dough. Shape the dough into smooth balls, about ¾ inch in diameter. (Each ball will make half of a "peach.") Arrange the dough balls 1 inch apart on buttered baking sheets.

8. Bake for 17 to 20 minutes, until the cookies are golden brown on the bottom. Transfer the cookies to racks to cool completely.

9. Use the tip of a small sharp knife to hollow out the cookies to make room for the filling. Starting in the center of the flat side, carefully turn the knife and rotate the cookie to make a hollow about 1-inch wide and ½-inch deep. Crumble the pieces and reserve 1½ cups of the cookie crumbs for the filling.

10. To make the filling, in a medium-size bowl, stir together the reserved cookie crumbs, the jam, nuts, melted chocolate, and orange juice until well blended.

11. To assemble, spoon the filling into the hollow in each cookie to form a "pit." Place the flat sides of two filled cookies together to form a "peach."

12. Brush half of each peach generously with water. Immediately roll in the red sugar for blush, patting the sugar onto the surface to make a thick coating.

13. Quickly brush the other half of each peach with water. Roll both sides of the peach in the yellow-orange sugar, patting the sugar onto the surface to make a generous coating. Set aside to dry. (For a heavier sugar coating, brush again with water and roll in sugar again once the first coating has dried.)

14. Insert a small piece of cinnamon stick into the top of each peach to make a stem. Garnish with a small leaf, if desired.

Angel Food Cake with Fluffy Frosting
(see recipe on page 132.)

SUNDAY

Sunday always feels different from the rest of the week, the world slowing down to the graciousness and leisure of a day of rest. It is the delicious chance we finally have to enjoy easy moments with those we love, to take time for that long-overdue conversation with best friends, to indulge in the solitary pleasure of a private reverie. In the pages that follow are desserts for all those small and quiet times that make Sunday remarkable ~ Grandmother's wicker basket holds a cherry cobbler for an impromptu picnic; a slice of lemon meringue pie piques the tastebuds as you pour over a favorite short story; a generous helping of moist vanilla pound cake serves as a nourishing companion on a sleepy boatride. Sunday is indeed a very special day, and these are just the desserts to make it even more so.

LEMON MERINGUE PIE

Makes 8 servings

PASTRY

½ recipe Old-Fashioned Dough
(page 199)

LEMON FILLING

1 cup granulated sugar

¼ cup plus 2 tablespoons
cornstarch

¼ teaspoon salt

4 large egg yolks

2 teaspoons grated lemon zest

½ cup freshly squeezed lemon
juice

3 tablespoons unsalted butter,
cut into bits

MERINGUE

4 large egg whites, at room
temperature

¼ teaspoon cream of tartar

Pinch of salt

½ cup superfine sugar

¾ teaspoon vanilla extract

1. Preheat the oven to 425°F. Set out a 9-inch pie plate.

2. Roll the pastry on a lightly floured surface into a 12-inch round. Fit the pastry into the pie plate and trim and flute the edge. Prick the pastry with a fork.

3. Line the pastry shell with a double thickness of foil and fill the foil with dried beans or pie weights. Place the pie plate on a baking sheet.

4. Bake the pastry for 15 minutes, then remove the foil and beans. Bake for 5 to 10 minutes longer, until lightly browned. Transfer to a rack to cool.

5. To make the lemon filling, in a heavy medium-size nonreactive saucepan, whisk together the granulated sugar, cornstarch, and salt until blended. Whisk in 1¾ cups of cold water until smooth.

6. Bring the mixture to a boil over medium heat, stirring constantly. Boil and stir for 1 minute, then remove the pan from the heat.

7. In a medium-size bowl, whisk the egg yolks. Gradually whisk in the hot sugar mixture, adding it several large spoonfuls at a time and whisking until fully

A don't-mess-with-me recipe that's as classic as it gets.

blended before adding more. Pour the mixture back into the same saucepan.

8. Bring the mixture to a boil over medium heat, stirring constantly. Cook and stir for 2 minutes then remove from the heat.

9. Add the lemon zest and juice and butter, stirring until the butter melts. Pour the filling into the pie shell and let it cool slightly while you make the meringue.

10. Preheat the oven to 350°F. In the large bowl of an electric mixer, at low speed, beat the egg whites, cream of tartar, and salt until foamy. Increase the mixer speed to high and beat until soft peaks start to form.

11. Gradually beat in the superfine sugar, 1 tablespoon at a time, beating until stiff, glossy peaks form when the beaters are lifted. Beat in the vanilla.

12. Using a large spoon, pile the meringue on top of the lemon filling, mounding it in the center and spreading it to the pastry edge. Make sure that there are no gaps and that the meringue is sealed to the pastry. With the back of a teaspoon, make swirls in the meringue.

13. Bake the pie for 15 to 20 minutes, until the meringue is golden brown. Transfer the pie to a rack and cool for at least 4 hours before serving, preferably on the same day that it is baked. Refrigerate any leftovers.

OLD ORIGINAL BOOKBINDER'S APPLE WALNUT PIE

Makes 8 servings

PASTRY

1¾ cups all-purpose flour

¼ cup granulated sugar

1 teaspoon ground cinnamon

½ cup (1 stick) cold unsalted butter, cut into bits

APPLE FILLING

1 cup granulated sugar

½ cup all-purpose flour

Pinch of salt

Two 8-ounce containers sour cream

2 large eggs, lightly beaten

2 teaspoons vanilla extract

6 medium-size tart apples, peeled, cored and sliced (8 cups)

STREUSEL TOPPING

½ cup packed light or dark brown sugar

½ cup granulated sugar

½ cup all-purpose flour

1 teaspoon ground cinnamon

Pinch of salt

½ cup (1 stick) unsalted butter, at room temperature

1 cup chopped walnuts

1. To make the pastry, in a large bowl, stir together the flour, granulated sugar, and cinnamon. With a pastry blender or two knives, cut in the butter until the mixture forms a coarse meal.

2. Gradually add 5 to 6 tablespoons of ice water (or a bit more if needed), tossing the mixture with a fork, until moistened. Gather the dough into a ball, shape it into a disk, and wrap the dough in plastic. Refrigerate 1 hour, or until chilled.

3. To make the apple filling, in a large bowl, stir together the granulated sugar, flour, and salt. Add the sour cream, eggs, and vanilla and stir until blended. Add the apples and mix gently until coated.

4. Preheat the oven to 450°F. Set out a 10-inch pie plate.

5. Roll the pastry on a well-floured work surface into a 13- to 14-inch round. Fit the pastry into the pie plate, trim the edge reserving the pastry scraps, and flute it

Philadelphia Sundays wouldn't be the same without Bookbinder's pie.

high, the filling is generous. Pour the filling into the pastry and place the pie on a baking sheet. Using a small knife, cut the pastry scraps into leaf shapes. Use the dull side of the knife to create veins and place the leaves on a baking sheet.

6. Bake the pie for 10 minutes, then reduce the oven temperature to 350°F. Bake for 30 minutes longer. Bake the pastry leaves for about 10 minutes, or until golden. Transfer the leaves to a rack to cool.

7. Meanwhile, make the streusel topping. In a medium-size bowl, mix the brown sugar, granulated sugar, flour, cinnamon, and salt. With a pastry blender or two knives, cut in the butter until the mixture is crumbly. Stir in the walnuts.

8. Crumble the topping evenly over the hot pie. Bake for 20 to 25 minutes longer, until the topping is set in the center and is lightly browned. Transfer the pie to a rack to cool completely. Cut the pie into wedges and serve garnished with the pastry leaves. Refrigerate any leftovers.

APPLE CLAFOUTIS

Makes 8 servings

A clafoutis is a custard-based fruit tart from the Limousin region of France. When baked, the custard batter puffs up and turns a deep golden brown. Traditionally, the rustic dessert is made with fresh, unpitted, sweet cherries. This fragrant apple and vanilla-scented clafoutis is an all-season variation on the original.

3 cups milk

1¼ cups granulated sugar

1 vanilla bean, split lengthwise

⅔ cup all-purpose flour

5 large eggs, beaten

1¼ pounds tart apples (3 or 4), peeled, cored, sliced and tossed with lemon juice

Confectioners' sugar, for garnish

1. Preheat the oven to 375°F. Generously butter a 10- by 2-inch layer-cake pan.

2. In a heavy medium-size saucepan, stir together the milk, granulated sugar, and vanilla bean. Bring to a boil over medium heat, stirring to dissolve the sugar. Reduce the heat to low and simmer gently for 2 minutes. Remove from the heat.

3. Put the flour in the large bowl of an electric mixer. With the mixer at medium speed, gradually add the eggs, ¼ cup at a time, beating after each addition until well blended Beat the batter until it is very smooth.

4. Remove the vanilla bean from the milk. Pour the milk into a pitcher and pour it into the batter, beating at medium speed until well blended. (The mixture will be very thin.) Pour the batter into the prepared pan. Evenly arrange the apple slices over the top of the batter.

5. Bake for 65 minutes, or until it is puffed, golden brown, and firm to the touch. Cool the clafoutis in its pan on a rack until warm.

6. Dust the clafoutis with confectioners' sugar, cut into wedges, and serve.

Custard infused with vanilla bean lends a deep flavor to apples.

CAFE VICTORIA'S APPLE DUMPLINGS

Makes 4 servings

If apple dumplings are on the table, there's a good chance that fall is in the air. These dumplings are unusual in that the apples are cored and filled with a mixture of Grand Marnier, nutmeg, and cinnamon-scented apple puree before being enclosed in the pastry. Decorated with pastry leaves and tied up with dough ribbons, the dumplings are baked until the apples are tender and the pastry is golden. Arrange them all in a row on a silver tray for the most impressive presentation.

APPLE FILLING

2 cups peeled and chopped apple

¼ cup packed light or dark brown sugar

2 tablespoons Grand Marnier

¼ teaspoon ground cinnamon

Pinch of ground nutmeg

Pinch of salt

½ tablespoon unsalted butter

APPLE DUMPLINGS

Four 7-ounce Golden Delicious apples

Two 17¼-ounce packages frozen puff pastry sheets (4 sheets total), thawed according to package directions

Sliced apples, strawberries and mint sprigs, for garnish

1. To make the apple filling, in a heavy medium-size saucepan, stir together the chopped apple, brown sugar, Grand Marnier, cinnamon, nutmeg, and salt. Bring to a boil over medium-high heat, stirring constantly. Reduce the heat to low. Cover and simmer, stirring occasionally, for 25 minutes, or until the apples are very tender and the mixture is thick.

2. Remove from the heat and stir in the butter until it is melted.

3. To make the dumplings, core the whole apples through the stem end leaving the bottoms intact. Hollow out the centers of the apples to make generous room for the filling. Peel the top third of the apples and spoon in the filling.

A sophisticated puff pastry version of the cozy, childhood classic.

4. Gently unfold a sheet of puff pastry on a floured work surface. Press the pastry together at two seams to seal and roll it into an 11-inch square.

5. Trim the pastry to an 8½- to 9-inch square, reserving the scraps for decorations. Repeat with the remaining three sheets of pastry. (Since apples come in many sizes, make sure the dough squares are large enough to completely enclose the apples when they are placed in the centers.) Cut decorative shapes such as leaves from the dough scraps, including 4 long ribbons of dough.

6. Preheat the oven to 350°F. Set out a jelly-roll pan.

7. Place each apple in the center of a dough square. Bring the corners of the pastry up and over the apples, pinch together the seams on the sides, and fold over ¼ inch. Pinch to seal. Fold back the tips of the dough corners on top of the apples to allow steam to escape. Tie a dough ribbon around the top of each apple, running the ribbon under the dough flaps to hold the flaps in place.

8. Brush the pastry cutouts with cold water and press them gently onto the apples as decoration. Place the apple bundles on the jelly-roll pan.

9. Bake for 40 to 50 minutes, until the apples are tender and the pastry is golden.

10. Transfer the hot apple dumplings to dessert plates. Garnish with apple slices, strawberries, and mint sprigs if desired, and serve.

ANGEL FOOD CAKE WITH FLUFFY FROSTING

(Photograph on page 122)

Makes 12 servings

At one time, angel food cake was a staple in every baker's repertoire. Its delicate flavor and crumb make it a good platform for richly flavored ice creams, sorbets, and fruits. The cake's ethereal texture and dramatic height are due to the very large number of stiffly beaten egg whites (the only leavener) folded into the batter.

ANGEL FOOD CAKE

1 cup cake flour

1½ cups sugar

1½ cups egg whites (about 12 large whites), at room temperature

1½ teaspoons cream of tartar

1½ teaspoons vanilla extract

½ teaspoon almond extract

Pinch of salt

FLUFFY FROSTING

1 cup sugar

⅓ cup light corn syrup

2 large egg whites, at room temperature

¼ teaspoon cream of tartar

½ teaspoon vanilla extract

Fresh berries, for garnish

1. Set one oven rack in the lowest position and preheat the oven to 300°F. Set out a 10-inch tube (or angel food cake) pan with a removable bottom. (Do not use a pan with a nonstick coating and do not butter the pan.)

2. To make the cake, sift together the flour and ¾ cup of the sugar several times.

3. In the large bowl of an electric mixer, at medium-high speed, beat the egg whites, cream of tartar, vanilla and almond extracts, and the salt until soft peaks begin to form.

4. Slowly add the remaining ¾ cup of sugar, beating until nearly stiff peaks form when the beaters are lifted, scraping the side of the bowl often.

5. A little at a time, sift the flour mixture over the beaten whites and fold it in with a large rubber spatula. Pour the batter into the pan and draw a knife through the batter to release any air bubbles.

6. Bake the cake on the bottom oven rack for 30 minutes. Then increase the oven temperature to 325°F and bake for 20 to 25 minutes longer, until the top springs back when the cake is gently touched. (The cake will not fill the pan.)

7. Invert the pan and cool the cake, upside down, and supported on a bottle inserted into the center of the cake pan tube, for 1½ to 2 hours, until the cake is completely cool.

8. Gently run a sharp knife around the inside edge of the pan and the center tube to release the cake. Invert the cake, and remove the pan sides by gently pressing on the bottom of the pan. Turn the cake right side up and run a knife around the bottom to loosen the cake. Invert the cake onto a serving plate and remove the bottom of the pan.

9. To make the frosting, in the top of a double boiler, combine the sugar, corn syrup, egg whites, and cream of tartar with 3 tablespoons of warm water. Using a portable electric mixer, at medium speed, beat for 1 minute to blend.

10. Place the pan over boiling water and cook over medium heat, beating constantly with the mixer at high speed for 7 minutes, or until peaks form and a candy or instant-read thermometer registers 160°F. Remove the pan from the boiling water.

11. Add the vanilla. Continue beating at high speed for 2 to 3 minutes, until a spreading consistency is achieved. (The frosting will have a soft marshmallow-like texture.) Use the frosting immediately.

12. Brush any loose crumbs off the cake with a dry pastry brush. With a thin metal spatula, spread the top and sides of the cake with the frosting.

13. Cut the cake into wedges with a serrated knife that has been dipped in warm water. Serve the cake accompanied by an assortment of fresh berries.

BLUEBERRY PIE

Makes 8 servings

Few things in life are as simple and satisfying as picking blueberries early on a summer's morning and turning that harvest into a sweet, juicy pie. In this recipe, the unusual inclusion of allspice and cloves adds richness and depth of flavor to the blueberries, and the very flaky crust provides a textural contrast. For a summery-looking top crust, roll out the pastry, then cut out freeform leaves (about two inches long) with a paring knife and create veins with the dull side of the knife. Arrange the leaves over the filling, slightly overlapping them, and "gluing" them to each other with a little cold water. The leaves can be brushed with a beaten whole egg to give them a deep golden color and rich sheen.

FLAKY PASTRY

2 cups all-purpose flour

½ teaspoon salt

¾ cup solid white vegetable shortening

BLUEBERRY FILLING

¾ cup packed light or dark brown sugar

¾ cup granulated sugar

¼ cup all-purpose flour

3 tablespoons quick-cooking tapioca

¼ teaspoon ground allspice

¼ teaspoon ground cloves

4 cups blueberries, or 20 ounces frozen blueberries, thawed, with juice

3 tablespoons blueberry or other berry-flavored liqueur

1. To make the flaky pastry, in a large bowl, stir together the flour and salt. With a pastry blender or two knives, cut the shortening into the flour until the mixture forms a coarse meal.

2. Add 6 to 7 tablespoons of ice water, one tablespoon at a time, tossing with a fork until the flour is moistened. Gather the dough into a ball and divide it into two-third and one-third portions. Shape each portion into a disk, wrap the dough in plastic, and refrigerate it while you prepare the filling.

From Sunday picnics to Church suppers, there isn't a better loved pie.

3. To make the blueberry filling, in a medium-size bowl, stir together the brown sugar, granulated sugar, flour, tapioca, allspice, and cloves until blended. Put the blueberries into a large bowl, pour the sugar and spice mixture over them, and mix gently. Drizzle with the liqueur and mix again.

4. Preheat the oven to 375°F. Set out a 9-inch pie plate.

5. Roll the larger piece of pastry on a floured surface into a 12-inch round. Fit the pastry into the pie plate. Spoon the blueberry filling into the pastry shell.

6. Roll the smaller piece of pastry into a 9½-inch round and place it on top of the filling. Trim and flute the edge. Make several slits in the top crust with a knife to allow the steam to escape. Place the pie plate on a baking sheet.

7. Bake the pie for 55 to 65 minutes, until the filling is bubbling and the crust is nicely browned. Transfer the pie to a rack and cool to room temperature.

PEACH SHORTCAKE

Makes 6 servings

At one time, angel food cake was a staple in every baker's repertoire. Its delicate flavor and crumb make it a good platform for richly flavored ice creams, sorbets, and fruits. The cake's ethereal texture and dramatic height are due to the very large number of stiffly beaten egg whites (the only leavener) folded into the batte

PEACH FILLING

3 cups peeled and thickly sliced peaches

2 tablespoons honey

1 tablespoon freshly squeezed lemon juice

SHORTCAKE BISCUITS

1 recipe Sweet Biscuit Dough (page 199), made with nutmeg

1 teaspoon granulated sugar

CREAM TOPPING

1 cup heavy cream

2 tablespoons confectioners' sugar

¼ teaspoon ground nutmeg

Mint sprigs, for garnish

1. To make the peach filling, in a medium-size bowl, toss together the peaches, honey, and lemon juice. Cover and refrigerate until you are ready to serve.

2. Preheat the oven to 425°F. Set out a baking sheet.

3. Roll the dough on a floured surface into a ½-inch thick round. With a floured 3-inch biscuit cutter, cut out six rounds. Arrange the biscuits 1 inch apart on the baking sheet. Sprinkle the tops with the granulated sugar.

4. Bake the biscuits for 12 minutes, or until they are golden brown. Transfer the biscuits to a rack to cool completely.

5. Meanwhile, make the cream topping. In the chilled medium-size bowl of an electric mixer, at high speed, beat the cream, confectioners' sugar, and nutmeg until stiff peaks form. Cover and refrigerate until you are ready to serve.

6. Split the biscuits in half horizontally. Place the biscuit bottoms on dessert plates. After setting aside a few slices for garnish, spoon the remaining peaches and

accumulated peach juices onto the biscuit bottoms. Top each with a dollop of the cream and cover with the biscuit tops.

7. Top the shortcakes with spoonfuls of cream and the reserved peach slices. Garnish with mint sprigs and serve. Refrigerate any leftovers.

When homey is elegant: fresh peaches, plain biscuits, and whipped cream.

Simple Flourishes When family and friends visit on Sunday, dinner becomes an occasion—and dessert is just time to make a statement. Here are some ideas:

• Garnish a frosted cake with flowers and edge it with dragees or leaves. (Pesticide-free.)

• Dust half of each dessert plate with confectioners' sugar and the other half with cocoa. Or dust the plates with confectioners' sugar, and then lay a stencil—cut with various-sized holes—and dust cocoa through the holes—polka dots have never been more elegant.

JOHN CLANCY'S POUND CAKE

Makes 8 to 10 servings

The recipe for this classic cake was developed by John Clancy, chef, cooking teacher, and New York restaurateur. Originally, pound cake recipes called for one pound each of butter, sugar, flour, and eggs, which produced a rich, moist, dense-textured cake. Over time however, the proportion of ingredients has been altered to produce a lighter, airier cake, more in keeping with modern preferences.

2 cups sifted all-purpose flour

¼ teaspoon cream of tartar

¼ teaspoon ground mace

¼ teaspoon salt

1 cup (2 sticks) unsalted butter, at room temperature

1⅔ cups sugar

2 tablespoons brandy

1 teaspoon vanilla extract

5 large eggs, at room temperature

1. Preheat the oven to 325°F. Butter a 9- by 5- by 3-inch loaf pan. Line the pan with waxed paper or parchment paper cut to fit and butter the paper.

2. Sift together the flour, cream of tartar, mace, and salt.

3. In the large bowl of an electric mixer, at medium-high speed, beat the butter until it is very creamy, about 2 minutes. Very gradually, add the sugar, beating until light and fluffy, about 5 minutes. Beat in the brandy and the vanilla.

4. Beat in the eggs, one at a time, beating well after each addition.

5. Reduce the mixer speed to low and gradually add the flour mixture, beating until just blended. Pour the batter into the prepared pan and smooth the top.

6. Bake the cake for 1 hour and 30 to 35 minutes, until a toothpick inserted in the center comes out clean.

7. Cool the cake in the pan on a rack for 10 minutes. Run a thin metal spatula around the edge of the cake to loosen it. Invert the cake onto the rack to cool completely. Peel off the paper and store the cake in an airtight container.

SOUR CHERRY COBBLER

Makes 9 servings

Cobblers are one of the all-time favorite American desserts. They are usually lightly sweetened fresh fruit, topped with generous dollops of rich biscuit dough, and baked until bubbling and golden. In this upside down version, sour cherries are scattered on top of an orange-scented batter and baked.

1 cup all-purpose flour

½ cup sugar, plus an additional ½ cup

Grated zest of 1 medium-size orange

1 teaspoon baking powder

½ teaspoon salt

4 tablespoons cold unsalted butter, cut into bits

½ cup milk

1 large egg

½ teaspoon vanilla extract

3 cups pitted fresh sour cherries, or one 16-ounce bag frozen sour cherries, thawed and drained

1 teaspoon ground nutmeg

1. Preheat the oven to 350°F. Butter an 8- by 8- by 2-inch baking dish.

2. In the medium-size bowl of an electric mixer, at low speed, mix the flour, ½ cup of the sugar, the orange zest, baking powder, and salt.

3. Increase the mixer speed to medium-low. Beat in the butter until the mixture forms a coarse meal.

4. In a 2-cup glass measure, whisk together the milk, egg, and vanilla. Make a well in the center of the dry ingredients and pour in the milk mixture. Increase the mixer speed to medium and beat the batter until it is fluffy.

5. Spread the batter in the prepared pan. Scatter the cherries evenly over the top of the batter. Combine the remaining ½ cup of sugar with the nutmeg and sprinkle it over the cherries.

6. Bake the cobbler for 40 minutes, or until a toothpick comes out clean. Serve warm or at room temperature.

A Venerable Table at Bookbinder's

Find a great seafood house and you'll usually find a great dessert menu. The seemingly odd affinity between sweet foods and denizens of the brine is deliciously proven everyday at Philadelphia's legendary Bookbinder's restaurant. Their menu of luscious homestyle desserts perfectly complements the simple, exquisitely prepared seafood and fish.

After a visit to the Benjamin Franklin Institute or the Liberty Bell, a dinner topped with an old-fashioned dessert keeps the history flowing. A restaurant that opened as the Civil War ended, Bookbinder's has been preparing their treasured recipes for so long that Philadelphians practically regard it as home cooking. Sarah and Sam Bookbinder started their cafe in 1865, whose plain brick walls and dark wooden floors reverberated with laughter and city gossip, much as they do today. As you scan your menu, a view of Philadelphia's culinary history rolls past in a selection of turn-of-the-century dishes. Prominent among them are their famous

Sundays in Philadelphia: sweet traditions.

desserts, including sweet strawberry shortcake, chocolate cheesecake, and coconut layer cake, all served in extra-generous portions.

Philadelphians have always preferred their foods simple, fresh, and abundant. That's the successful Bookbinders's food philosophy. A taste of their Old Original Bookbinder's Apple Walnut Pie feels just like a visit to an old farmhouse kitchen. The meltingly sweet butter crust is piled high with cups and cups of apples and sour cream, then thickly coated with the richest walnut streusel topping.

Not ones to be left in the sawdust, Bookbinder's pastry chefs infuse their classic dessert offerings with new treats such as the glamorous Peanut Butter Pie. Quiet sighs of pleasure greet the first forkful of this beauty: drifting atop the creamiest peanut butter filling, a heavenly downfall of sweet whipped cream piles into deep banks.

For a Sunday you want to never end, order up pots of Bookbinder's hearty coffee, sit back and enjoy the traditions of a cherished American culinary institution.

BREAD AND BUTTER PUDDING WITH CINNAMON CREAM

Makes 6 servings

BREAD AND BUTTER PUDDING

4 small white rolls, such as cloverleaf (5 ounces total)

3 tablespoons unsalted butter, at room temperature

3 tablespoons raisins, plumped in hot water for 5 minutes

1¼ cups heavy cream

1 cup milk

1 vanilla bean

3 large eggs

⅔ cup granulated sugar

1½ tablespoons apricot jam

CINNAMON CREAM

1¼ cups milk

½ cup heavy cream

1 cinnamon stick

4 large egg yolks

⅓ cup granulated sugar

Confectioners' sugar, for garnish

1. Preheat the oven to 350°F. Butter an 8- by 1½-inch round baking dish.

2. To make the bread and butter pudding, cut the rolls into thin slices and butter the slices on one side. Arrange the bread slices, buttered side up and slightly overlapping in the prepared baking dish. Sprinkle a layer of raisins in between each layer of bread, ending with a layer of bread slices.

3. In a medium-size saucepan, over medium heat, bring the cream, milk, and vanilla bean to a boil. Remove from the heat.

4. In a medium-size bowl, whisk together the eggs and granulated sugar. Remove the vanilla bean from the milk mixture, and gradually whisk the milk mixture into the eggs. Pour the custard evenly over the bread.

5. Bake for 45 to 50 minutes, until evenly puffed and set in the center.

6. Gently spread the apricot jam on top of the hot pudding. Place the pudding on a rack and let it stand until warm.

7. Meanwhile, make the cinnamon cream. In a small saucepan, over medium heat, bring the milk, cream, and cinnamon stick to a boil. Remove from the heat, and cover with plastic wrap to keep the mixture warm.

8. In the medium-size bowl of an electric mixer, at high speed, beat the egg yolks and granulated sugar until they are thick and pale yellow, about 6 minutes.

9. Remove the cinnamon stick from the milk. With the mixer at low speed, slowly pour the milk into the yolks, beating until they are blended. Pour into a nonreactive medium-size heavy saucepan.

10. Place the saucepan over medium heat and cook, stirring constantly, until the mixture coats a wooden spoon. Do not let it boil. Immediately remove the sauce from the heat and pour into a sauceboat.

11. Lightly dust the bread pudding with confectioners' sugar, cut into wedges, and serve accompanied by the warm cinnamon cream.

Four Steps To Silky Custard

Silky smooth custard is one of life's simple pleasures. The plainest cake turns elegant when surrounded by a pool of vanilla-scented crème anglaise. It's easy to prepare a perfect custard ~ here are a few simple tips.

• Always cook the custard in a heavy-bottomed nonreactive saucepan.

• Custard should be stirred constantly as it cooks with a wooden spoon to avoid scratching the bottom of the pan.

• A custard should never be allowed to boil. Custards are properly thickened at about 165°F on an instant-read thermometer.

• If the custard begins to curdle, immediately pour it into a metal bowl and set it into a large bowl of ice water, stirring constantly, until the sauce is cool to the touch. Pour the custard through a fine-mesh strainer and it is then ready to use.

Meringue Basket With Berries

(recipe on page 156)

CELEBRATIONS

For those truly special moments in our lives when we gather family and friends to share in life's joys, mark milestones, praise personal achievements, and strengthen our deepest ties, only the very best will do. Whether we're celebrating a granddaughter's christening, a friend's graduation from college, a professional triumph, or a formal holiday, desserts seem to make life's special occasions even sweeter and more joyful. In this chapter are just such festive creations, something to suit every event and every size gathering, from an intimate anniversary toast to a wedding feast for the entire family. We offer buttery heart cookies iced with pink to please the littlest valentine; a regal currant and raisin cake to accentuate the joy of Christmas; a simple strawberry rhubarb custard pie to pay homage to the first day of spring.

GINGER HEART COOKIES

Makes about 9 dozen cookies

COOKIES

1 tablespoon baking soda

1½ tablespoons ground ginger

1 tablespoon ground cinnamon

1 tablespoon ground cloves

2½ cups granulated sugar

½ cup (1 stick) unsalted butter

½ cup dark corn syrup

½ cup heavy cream

1 large egg yolk

5 cups all-purpose flour

ICING

1 cup confectioners' sugar

5 to 6 teaspoons heavy cream

Liquid food coloring

1. Line a baking sheet with plastic wrap.

2. To make the cookies, in a small dish, stir together the baking soda, the ginger, cinnamon, and cloves.

3. In a medium-size saucepan, place the granulated sugar, butter, and corn syrup. Bring to a boil over medium heat, stirring until the butter melts and the sugar dissolves. Pour the mixture into the large bowl of an electric mixer.

4. With the mixer at medium speed, slowly beat in the cream until it is blended. Add the spice mixture and the egg yolk and beat until they are well blended.

5. Reduce the mixer speed to low. Add 4 cups of the flour, one cup at a time, beating just until blended after each addition. Stir in the remaining 1 cup of flour by hand until a fairly firm smooth dough has formed.

6. Shape the dough into an 11- by 8-inch rectangle on the lined baking sheet. Cover the dough with plastic wrap and refrigerate overnight.

7. Remove the dough from the refrigerator about 2 hours before you plan to start baking. The dough needs to be at room temperature for the easiest handling.

8. Preheat the oven to 350°F. Line several baking sheets with parchment paper.

9. Divide the dough into four equal pieces. Roll each piece of dough on a floured surface into a 16- by 12-inch rectangle, about ⅛ inch thick. Cut out cookies with a lightly floured heart-shaped cutter. Using a pancake spatula, transfer the

Easy handling ginger cookies may be decorated for any occasion.

cookies to the prepared baking sheets spacing them about 1 inch apart.

10. Bake the cookies for 5 to 8 minutes, until they are puffed. (They will settle as they cool.) Cool them slightly on the baking sheets (so that the cookies don't break) before transferring the cookies to racks to cool completely.

11. To make the icing, in a small bowl, stir about ⅓ cup of the confectioners' sugar with enough of the cream to make a piping consistency. (The icing will just hold its shape when it is dropped from the tip of a spoon.) Tint the icing with food coloring as desired. Spoon the icing into a small pastry bag fitted with a narrow plain tip and pipe decorative swirls, lines, and dots onto the cookies.

12. Decorate all the cookies with the remaining confectioners' sugar and cream. It will take several batches of icing to decorate all of the cookies, but make small batches of icing because this icing hardens very quickly.

WHITE CHOCOLATE MUFFINS

Makes 15 muffins

Looks are deceiving ~ these muffins may look like plain vanilla, but they're actually a richly flavored combination of white chocolate and orange. Serve them with warm mugs of tea, or hot chocolate topped with a spoonful of lightly whipped cream and a sprinkle of white chocolate shavings.

½ cup frozen orange juice concentrate, thawed (not diluted)

½ cup milk

1 large egg, at room temperature

¼ cup vegetable oil

2 cups all-purpose flour

⅓ cup coarsely grated white chocolate (about 1½ ounces)

¼ cup ground almonds

¼ cup sugar

2 tablespoons baking powder

1. Preheat the oven to 400°F. Butter fifteen 2½-inch muffin cups or line muffin tins with paper or foil baking cups.
2. In a medium-size bowl, whisk together the orange juice concentrate, milk, egg, and oil until they are well blended.
3. In a large bowl, stir together the flour, chocolate, almonds, sugar, and baking powder. Make a well in the center of the flour mixture.
4. Pour the milk mixture into the well and stir the ingredients together until just moistened. Do not overmix the batter or the muffins will be tough. Spoon the batter into the prepared muffin cups, filling them three-quarters full.
5. Bake the muffins for 15 to 18 minutes, until the tops are golden brown and a toothpick inserted in the center comes out clean. Turn the muffins out of the pans onto racks and serve warm.

Brunch, lunch, or tea, these moist muffins make elegant holiday fare.

A party dessert par excellence, requiring extra preparation time.

PARIS BREST

Makes 8 to 10 servings

Paris Brest is a traditional French dessert, a combination of choux pastry, whipped cream, and almonds. The choux paste is piped into a ring shape and baked. The ring is then sliced horizontally and filled with praline-flavored whipped cream. It's not advisable to make this dessert on a humid day ~ the pastry ring will be damp and the praline will not crisp properly. You can, however, make the praline several days ahead and store it in a tightly covered jar.

PASTRY RING

½ cup (1 stick) unsalted butter, cut into bits

1 cup all-purpose flour

Pinch of salt

5 large eggs, 1 of them lightly beaten

¼ cup sliced unblanched almonds

Confectioners' sugar, for garnish

PRALINE

½ cup granulated sugar

½ cup sliced unblanched almonds

PRALINE CREAM FILLING

2 cups heavy cream

¼ cup praline liqueur

1. Lightly butter a baking sheet and dust it with flour, shaking off the excess. Using your finger, draw a 7-inch diameter circle in the center of the sheet.

2. To make the pastry ring, place the butter in a medium-size heavy saucepan with 1 cup of water. Bring to a boil over medium-high heat, stirring often, until the butter is melted.

3. Reduce the heat to medium-low and add the flour and salt all at once. Cook, stirring vigorously with a wooden spoon for 1 minute, or until the mixture leaves the side of the pan and forms a ball.

4. Preheat the oven to 400°F.

5. Remove from the heat and let the mixture cool for 5 minutes. Add the 4 whole eggs, one at a time, beating well after each addition to form a shiny dough.

6. Spoon the dough into a pastry bag fitted with a ¾-inch plain tip. Pipe the dough along the outside of the circle you've marked on the baking sheet. Pipe one or two additional dough rings on top of the first one.

7. Brush the dough ring with the beaten egg, and sprinkle with the almonds. Sift confectioners' sugar over the almonds and dough.

8. Bake for 15 minutes. Reduce the oven temperature to 350°F and bake for 35 minutes longer, or until the pastry ring is puffed and browned. Transfer to a rack to cool the pastry completely.

9. With a long serrated knife, carefully slice the pastry ring in half horizontally. Scoop out the damp webbing from the center with a fork, leaving a shell.

10. To make the praline, butter a baking sheet. In a heavy 8½-inch skillet, combine the granulated sugar and almonds. Place over medium-low heat and cook until the sugar melts, shaking the pan occasionally (do not stir). When the sugar has melted and turned an even golden brown, carefully pour the syrup onto the prepared baking sheet. Let the praline cool completely.

11. Break the praline into small pieces and pulverize in a food processor. Store in an airtight container until you are ready to use it.

12. To make the praline cream filling, in the large bowl of an electric mixer, at medium speed, beat the cream until soft peaks form. Gradually add the praline liqueur, beating until stiff peaks form. Fold in the crushed praline.

13. To assemble, place the bottom half of the pastry ring on a serving plate. Fit a pastry bag with a large star tip and fill it with the cream filling. Pipe the filling into the bottom of the pastry ring. Replace the top of the pastry ring and lightly sift confectioners' sugar over the top.

14. Serve the Paris Brest at once or refrigerate for up to one hour before serving. Refrigerate any leftovers.

STRAWBERRY RHUBARB CUSTARD PIE

Makes 8 servings

1 recipe Charlotte's Pie Crust
(page 198)

¾ cup sugar, plus additional for
sprinkling

1 tablespoon cornstarch

⅛ teaspoon ground nutmeg

Pinch of salt

2 large eggs

⅓ cup half-and-half, plus
1 tablespoon for the glaze

2 tablespoons unsalted butter,
melted

½ pound rhubarb, chopped
(2 cups)

2 cups sliced strawberries

1. Roll two-thirds of the pie crust on a floured surface into a 12-inch round. Fit the pastry into a 9-inch pie plate.

2. Roll the remaining pastry into a 10-inch round. Cut into ¾-inch wide strips for the lattice top. Cover the pastry strips with plastic wrap and set them aside.

3. Preheat the oven to 400°F.

4. In a small bowl, stir together the sugar, cornstarch, nutmeg, and salt.

5. In a large bowl, thoroughly whisk the eggs. Whisk in the sugar mixture, then the half-and-half and butter, whisking until the mixture is blended. Add the rhubarb and strawberries and toss to mix. Pour the filling into the pie shell.

6. Crisscross the pastry strips in a lattice pattern over the top of the pie, sealing the strips at the edge. Fold the pastry edge over and crimp decoratively to seal.

7. Brush the pastry with the 1 tablespoon of half-and-half and sprinkle with sugar.

8. Bake for 20 minutes. Reduce the oven temperature to 350°F and bake for 30 to 35 minutes longer, until the filling is set in the center.

9. Transfer the pie to a rack to cool. Refrigerate any leftovers.

La Fête de Noël: Chez Suzelle

Alsace is the region in northeast France next to the German border that's legendary for its devotion to fine dining. Nowhere in Alsace is this tradition more celebrated than in the centuries-old city of Strasbourg. Snuggled in the historic old quarter deep inside the walls of this fortress town is Chez Suzelle. Where dining is a pleasure never to be hurried—especially during holiday time when the desserts and sweets of a traditional Fête de Noël bring people together.

To savor the essence of an Alsatian Christmas celebration, friends old and new make their way to Odette Jung's cozy tearoom where

Dressed for Père Noël, Chez Suzelle glows at twilight time.

favorite holiday cakes, confections, and bobons join a cast of star performers. A light cheese tart, made with farmer's cheese and crème fraîche, looks irresistible perched high on a footed cake stand. An assortment of Chez Suzelle's signature fruit tarts try to outshine each other as mountains of sugar-glazed fruit pile up: blueberries, gooseberries, or the famous apple tarts laced with almond streusel topping.

Against the backdrop of its 1670 building, Chez Suzelle seems like a French fairy tale decorated with the Alsatian antiques Odette Jung collects. Comfortable folk furniture encourages lingering—perhaps to pen a journal or practice the local dialect. Bouquets of dried flowers are hung from dark ceiling timbers and fragrant greens are tucked everywhere. It's so spirited, even the waitresses are dressed in embroidered folk costumes.

Surrounded by flickering candlelight, the romance of the season feels even more palpable as tray after tray of goodies arrive from the kitchen. Greeted like old friends, Odette's celestial meringues, light as angel's hair, wait to be smothered under a pool of traditional custard sauce, so popular in Europe. A beautifully decorated slice of Odette's chocolate cake is delicious down to its last moist crumb. Recipes recorded in her hand-written cookbook she shares with guests reveal Odette's generous way with butter, cream, and seasonings.

MERINGUE BASKET WITH BERRIES

(PHOTOGRAPH ON PAGE 156)

Makes 6 servings

MERINGUE SHELL

6 large egg whites, at room temperature

Pinch of salt

1½ cups superfine sugar

DECORATIONS

4 large egg whites, at room temperature

1 cup superfine sugar

CREAM FILLING

1 cup heavy cream

2 tablespoons granulated sugar

1 tablespoon raspberry liqueur

3 to 4 cups raspberries, blackberries or blueberries

Confectioners' sugar and mint leaves, for garnish

1. Preheat the oven to 180°F. Butter and flour two baking sheets. With a finger or with the blunt end of a bamboo skewer, mark two 7-inch circles on each baking sheet using an inverted bowl or cake pan as a guide.

2. To make the meringue shell, in the large bowl of an electric mixer, at high speed, beat the egg whites and salt until soft peaks form. Gradually add the superfine sugar and beat until the egg whites are very stiff and glossy.

3. Fit a pastry bag with a ½-inch plain tip and fill the bag with the meringue. To make the base of the meringue basket, pipe concentric circles of meringue onto one of the marked circles, filling in the circle completely. Gently smooth the piped meringue with a thin metal spatula to make the base even.

4. On each of the three remaining outlined circles, pipe two rings of meringue, one on top of the other, using the outlines as a guide. The rings should be about 1¼ inches tall and straight sided.

5. Bake the meringue base and rings for 2 hours. Place the baking sheets on racks and let the meringues cool completely.

6. Loosen the meringue base and rings from the baking sheets using a thin metal

spatula. Place the meringue base on a rack set over a baking sheet.

7. To make the meringue decorations, preheat the oven to 180°F. In the large bowl of the mixer, at high speed, beat the egg whites until soft peaks form. Gradually add the superfine sugar and beat until very stiff and glossy.

8. Again, fit the pastry bag with the ½-inch plain tip. Fill the bag with some of the meringue and pipe dots of meringue along the edge of the baked meringue base. Carefully place the meringue rings on top of the base "cementing" each ring with dots of meringue. This will form the shell of the meringue basket.

9. "Frost" the outside of the shell with more of the meringue, using a thin metal spatula. Then, using a small plain tip, pipe lines of meringue going up and down on the outside of the basket. Lastly, pipe alternating horizontal lines to resemble a "basketweave" pattern.

10. Bake the meringue basket on the rack set on the baking sheet for 2 hours. The meringue basket should be crisp and dry, but not browned. Remove from the oven and let the meringue basket cool on its rack.

11. Just before serving, make the cream filling. In the small chilled bowl of the mixer, at high speed, beat the cream until it begins to thicken. Gradually add the granulated sugar and the raspberry liqueur, beating until soft peaks form.

12. Spoon the cream filling into the meringue basket and top with the berries. Dust with confectioners' sugar, garnish with mint leaves, and serve.

A high level of artistry is behind this innocent-looking dessert.

P U M P K I N   T A R T
W I T H   C R A N B E R R Y   F O O L

Makes 8 to 10 servings

PASTRY

1¾ cups all-purpose flour

⅔ cup (1 stick) plus 2⅔ tablespoons cold unsalted butter, cut into bits

CRANBERRY RELISH

One 12-ounce package fresh cranberries, sorted and rinsed

½ cup sugar

½ cup orange marmalade

PUMPKIN FILLING

2 large eggs

1 large egg yolk

1 cup canned solid-pack pumpkin puree

1 cup half-and-half

½ cup sugar

1 tablespoon grated orange zest

3 tablespoons freshly squeezed orange juice

3 tablespoons molasses

1 teaspoon ground cinnamon

¼ teaspoon freshly grated nutmeg

CRANBERRY FOOL

1 cup heavy cream

2 tablespoons sugar

⅓ cup Cranberry Relish (see recipe)

Pesticide-free pansies, for garnish

1. To make the pastry, in a food processor, put the flour and butter and pulse several times until the mixture forms a coarse meal.

2. With the processor running, add 4 to 5 tablespoons ice water and process until the dough pulls away from the side of the bowl and forms a ball. Shape the dough into a disk, wrap in plastic, and refrigerate for 1 hour, or until the dough is well chilled.

3. To make the cranberry relish, in the food processor, pulse the cranberries several times until they are finely chopped, but not pureed.

Autumn colors unite recipes from two great countries in one pie.

4. Transfer the cranberries to a medium-size bowl and stir in the sugar and the orange marmalade until well blended. Cover and refrigerate until ready to use.

5. Next make the pumpkin filling. Using the large bowl of an electric mixer, at medium speed, beat the eggs and egg yolk until they are foamy. Reduce the mixer speed to medium-low, and add the pumpkin, half-and-half, sugar, orange zest and juice, molasses, cinnamon, and nutmeg. Beat until blended.

6. Preheat the oven to 350°F. Set out a 10-inch tart pan.

7. Roll the pastry on a floured surface into a 14-inch round. Fit the pastry into the tart pan. Trim the pastry 1 inch higher than the rim of the pan and fold the pastry over to make a double thickness of dough just above the top of the pan. Press the pastry against the side of the tart pan to seal the layers together. Place the tart pan on a baking sheet and pour in the pumpkin filling.

8. Bake for 1 hour, or until a metal skewer inserted off-center comes out clean. Transfer the tart to a rack to cool completely.

9. No more than an hour before serving time, make the cranberry fool. In the chilled medium-size bowl of the mixer, at high speed, beat the cream and sugar until stiff peaks form. Fold in ⅓ cup of the cranberry relish. Cover and refrigerate until you are ready to serve.

10. Cut the tart into wedges and serve, garnished with pansies, and accompanied by the cranberry fool and additional cranberry relish. Refrigerate any leftovers.

For true Southern flavor, make this classic with Georgia pecans.

RUM PECAN PIE

Makes 8 servings

BUTTER PASTRY

1⅓ cups all-purpose flour

½ cup (1 stick) cold unsalted
butter, cut into bits

¼ teaspoon salt

PECAN FILLING

1 cup packed light or dark
brown sugar

½ cup granulated sugar

5 tablespoons unsalted butter,
at room temperature

4 large eggs, at room
temperature

2 tablespoons all-purpose flour

1 tablespoon dark rum

1 tablespoon brandy

1½ teaspoons vanilla extract

½ teaspoon salt

1½ cups pecan halves

1. To make the butter pastry, in a food processor, put the flour, butter, and salt. Pulse the mixture several times until coarse crumbs form.

2. With the processor running, gradually add 3 to 5 tablespoons of ice water and process until the dough pulls away from the side of the bowl and forms a ball. Shape the dough into a disk, wrap in plastic, and refrigerate for about 1 hour.

3. Preheat the oven to 350°F. Set out a 9-inch pie plate.

4. Roll the dough on a lightly floured surface into a 13-inch round. Fit the dough into the pie plate and trim and flute the pastry to make a high rim.

5. To make the pecan filling, in the medium-size bowl of an electric mixer, at medium speed, beat the brown sugar, granulated sugar, and butter until the mixture is fluffy and well blended.

6. Add the eggs, one at a time, beating well after each addition. Beat in the flour, rum, brandy, vanilla, and salt until they are blended. Stir in the pecans.

7. Pour the filling into the pie shell, and place the pie plate on a baking sheet.

8. Bake for 50 to 60 minutes, until the filling is set in the center and a toothpick inserted off-center comes out clean. Transfer the pie to a rack to cool.

PUMPKIN CHEESECAKE

Makes 10 to 12 servings

Rich with the flavors of pumpkin, pecans, and bourbon, this cheesecake is a tribute to America's bounty. Because it is very rich, you may want to offer your guests a lighter dessert, such as poached pears or apples, as well. Prepare the cheesecake the day before you plan to serve it so the flavors have a chance to soften and develop.

PECAN CRUST

¾ cup graham cracker crumbs

½ cup finely chopped pecans

¼ cup granulated sugar

¼ cup packed light or dark brown sugar

4 tablespoons unsalted butter, melted and cooled

PUMPKIN FILLING

Three 8-ounce packages cream cheese, at room temperature

½ cup granulated sugar

½ cup packed light or dark brown sugar

1½ cups canned solid-pack pumpkin puree

3 large eggs, at room temperature

2 tablespoons heavy cream

1 tablespoon bourbon

1 teaspoon vanilla extract

1 tablespoon cornstarch

1½ teaspoons ground cinnamon

½ teaspoon salt

½ teaspoon ground ginger

½ teaspoon freshly grated nutmeg

BOURBON CREAM TOPPING

1½ cups sour cream

3 tablespoons granulated sugar

1½ tablespoons bourbon

1. To make the pecan crust, in a large bowl, mix the graham cracker crumbs, pecans, granulated sugar, brown sugar, and butter until they are well blended.
2. Butter a 9-inch springform pan. Press the crumb mixture into the bottom and ½ inch up the sides of the pan. Refrigerate for 1 hour, or until firm.
3. Preheat the oven to 350°F.

From Roman times on, cheesecake is it. Pumpkin is a rich variation.

4. Next make the pumpkin filling. Using the large bowl of an electric mixer, at medium-high speed, beat the cream cheese, granulated sugar, and brown sugar until the mixture is smooth and fluffy. Reduce the mixer speed to medium and beat in the pumpkin until blended.

5. Beat in the eggs, cream, bourbon, and vanilla until the mixture is smooth. Put the cornstarch, cinnamon, salt, ginger, and nutmeg in a small strainer and sift it over the batter. Beat just until mixed, then pour the filling into the chilled crust and place the pan on a baking sheet.

6. Bake for 60 to 70 minutes, until the cheesecake is set and a toothpick inserted in the center comes out clean. Let the cake cool in the pan on a rack for 5 minutes.

7. Toward the end of the baking time, make the bourbon cream topping. In a medium-size bowl, stir together the sour cream, granulated sugar, and bourbon until they are blended. Spread over the top of the hot cheesecake.

8. Bake the cheesecake for 5 minutes longer, then transfer to a rack and cool to lukewarm. Cover the cheesecake loosely with foil and refrigerate overnight before serving. Refrigerate any leftovers.

DUTCH APPLE TART

Makes 8 servings

This tall, handsome tart is lovely when it is served still warm with Crème Anglaise (page 195) or butter pecan ice cream. A tart, crisp apple such as Granny Smith, Newton Pippin, Winesap, or Empire would be the best choice here.

BUTTERMILK CRUST

2½ cups all-purpose flour

2 tablespoons sugar

2 teaspoons baking powder

1 teaspoon salt

1 cup (2 sticks) unsalted butter, at room temperature

2 large egg yolks

¼ cup buttermilk

CRUMB TOPPING

½ cup sugar

⅓ cup all-purpose flour

1 teaspoon ground cinnamon

4 tablespoons unsalted butter, at room temperature

8 small tart apples (about 3 pounds), peeled, cored and sliced

Strawberries, for garnish

1. To make the buttermilk crust, in a large bowl, mix the flour, sugar, baking powder, and salt. Set out a 9-inch springform pan.

2. With a pastry blender or two knives, cut in the butter and egg yolks until the mixture forms coarse crumbs. Gradually drizzle the buttermilk over the crumb mixture, tossing with a fork, until it is moistened and a dough forms.

3. Gather the dough into a ball and shape it into a disk. Press the dough onto the bottom and halfway up the side of the springform pan.

4. Preheat the oven to 350°F.

5. To make the crumb topping, in a medium-size bowl, stir together the sugar, flour, and cinnamon. With a pastry blender or two knives, cut in the butter until the mixture is well blended.

6. Pile the apple slices into the crust, mounding them higher in the center and

A delicious change for Thanksgiving, a towering tart with crumbs.

allowing apples to extend above the crust at the sides. (The apples will settle during baking.) Sprinkle the apples evenly with the crumb topping, and place the springform pan on a baking sheet.

7. Bake the tart for 1¼ to 1½ hours, until the topping is browned and the apples are tender. Let the tart cool in its pan on a rack. Run a thin metal spatula around the edge of the pan to loosen the tart and remove the pan sides.

8. Transfer the tart to a serving plate and garnish with strawberries.

BRANDIED PUMPKIN PIE

Makes 8 servings

PÂTE BRISÉE

1¾ cups all-purpose flour

¼ teaspoon salt

½ cup (1 stick) cold unsalted
  butter, cut into bits

3 tablespoons solid white
  vegetable shortening, chilled

PUMPKIN FILLING

¾ cup packed dark brown sugar

¼ cup granulated sugar

1 tablespoon all-purpose flour

1½ teaspoons ground
  cinnamon

1 teaspoon ground ginger

¼ teaspoon ground cloves

¼ teaspoon freshly grated
  nutmeg

¼ teaspoon salt

One 16-ounce can solid-pack
  pumpkin puree

1 tablespoon molasses

3 large eggs

1¾ cups half-and-half

2 tablespoons brandy

1. To make the pâte brisée, in a medium-size bowl, together stir the flour and salt. With a pastry blender or two knives, cut in the butter and shortening until the mixture forms a coarse meal.

2. Gradually sprinkle in 4 to 5 tablespoons of ice water, tossing the mixture with a fork until it is all moistened. Gather the dough into a ball, shape it into a disk, and dust it with flour. Wrap the dough in plastic and refrigerate for at least 1 hour, or until chilled.

3. Roll the dough on a lightly floured surface into a 13- to 14-inch round. Fit the dough into a 10-inch pie plate. Trim the pastry, reserving the pastry scraps, and flute the pie to make a high edge. Prick the pastry shell all over with a fork, then cover, and refrigerate for 1 hour. Cut the pastry scraps into maple leaf shapes using a small knife. Use the dull side of the knife to create veins. Place the pastry leaves on a baking sheet and refrigerate.

4. Preheat the oven to 400°F. Line the pastry shell with a double thickness of foil.

From early Colonists to today, Americans have adored pumpkin pie.

Fill the foil with dried beans or pie weights. Bake for 10 minutes, remove the foil and beans, and bake for another 10 minutes, or until the pastry shell is lightly browned. Transfer to a rack to cool completely.

5. Reduce the oven temperature to 375°F.

6. To make the pumpkin filling, in a large bowl, stir together the brown sugar, granulated sugar, flour, cinnamon, ginger, cloves, nutmeg, and salt. Stir in the pumpkin and molasses until blended well.

7. In the small bowl of an electric mixer, at medium speed, beat the eggs until they are frothy. Reduce the mixer speed to low. Gradually beat in the half-and-half and brandy until they are blended. Stir into the pumpkin mixture.

8. Pour the pumpkin filling into the pie shell.

9. Bake for 60 to 65 minutes, until the filling is set and a toothpick inserted off-center comes out clean. Transfer to a rack to cool. Bake the pastry leaves for 10 minutes, or until light golden, then transfer to a rack to cool. Cut the pie into wedges and serve garnished with the maple pastry leaves.

CHRISTMAS CAKE

Makes 20 servings

Wonderfully Dickensian, Christmas cake evokes everything that's traditional about this holiday. The flavors need time to mellow, so once the cake has cooled, wrap it well and keep it in a cool spot for at least two weeks. Cut it into thin slices and serve with Crème Anglaise (page 195) or Hard Sauce (page 196).

3¼ cups all-purpose flour

1½ teaspoons pumpkin-pie spice

1½ cups (3 sticks) unsalted butter, at room temperature

1⅔ cups packed light or dark brown sugar

6 large eggs, at room temperature

4 cups dried currants (1 pound plus 6 ounces)

1⅓ cups golden raisins (8 ounces)

1⅓ cups dark raisins (8 ounces)

¾ cup candied cherries (5 ounces)

⅔ cup chopped candied orange and lemon peel

1 cup slivered almonds (4 ounces)

Grated zest and juice of 1 large lemon

1 tablespoon molasses

1. Arrange one rack in the bottom third of the oven. Preheat the oven to 300°F. Butter a 10-inch springform pan. Line the bottom of the pan with a double thickness of waxed paper cut to fit and butter the paper. Dust the pan with flour, shaking out the excess.

2. In a large bowl, stir together the flour and pumpkin-pie spice.

3. In the large bowl of an electric mixer, at medium-high speed, beat the butter until it is creamy. Gradually add the brown sugar, beating until the mixture is light and fluffy, scraping the side of the bowl often.

4. Add the eggs, one at a time, beating well, and adding a spoonful of the flour mixture after each addition. Reduce the mixer speed to low, and gradually mix

Endowed with a pantry-full of fruit, this cake is a wonderful gift.

in the remaining flour. Pour the batter into a very large bowl.

5. Stir in the currants, golden and dark raisins, cherries, candied peel, almonds, lemon zest and juice, and molasses, beating until just blended. Do not overmix. Pour the batter into the prepared pan and spread evenly. Form a 1-inch hollow in the center of the batter and place the pan on a baking sheet.

6. Bake in the bottom third of the oven for 2 to 2¼ hours, until the cake is firm to the touch and a toothpick inserted off-center comes out clean. (The hollow in the center of the cake will fill as it bakes.)

7. Let the cake cool in the pan on a rack for 10 minutes, then run a thin metal spatula around the edge of the pan to loosen the cake and remove the pan sides. Cool the cake completely on the rack. Invert the cake, remove the bottom of the pan, and peel off the paper. Wrap the cake in plastic and overwrap in foil. Store in a cool spot for at least two weeks before serving.

Tea at the Royal Crescent Hotel

Amid fine furniture and old portraits, a traditional teatime unfolds at the handsome Royal Crescent Hotel in Bath, England. Sitting next to a crackling fire in the hotel's beautifully appointed drawing room, one feels transported to the mid-nineteenth century. It was then that teatime became a beloved part of everyday British life. Victorian ladies, dressed in tea gowns, would join men just returned from a day's sport in the country-side . . . laughter floated across tables . . . groups of comfortable chairs encouraged long chats or an enchanted hour devoted to a book or journal.

In our day, dress may be less formal but, at the Royal Crescent Hotel, the trappings of teatime remain the same. Multi-tiered dessert stands display an abundance of classic English cakes and savories, each too tempting to resist. Plates of scones, strewn with currants and fruit, beg to be slathered with homemade preserves and dabs of fresh English clotted cream. Steaming cups of tea, poured from silver Georgian teapots, soon lift the spirits and the senses.

Beneath tapestries and fine prints, beyond the candle glow and firelight, magnificently paneled walls reveal the noble lineage of this townhouse. Reposing regally atop a hill, it was completed in 1775 as a residence for King George III's brother.

Soothing as a Royal Crescent tea is at all times of year, it is perhaps at Christmas that the Georgian mansion shines most brightly. Serving plates, tucked with sprigs of fresh holly and ivy, satisfy holiday yearnings with favorites from the past. Rich Christmas cake, chock-full of currants and nuts, is clad with marzipan. Sugar-glazed fruits, precious to the Victorians, glisten like new-fallen snow. To encourage guests to sample every delight, trays are heaped with miniature-sized classics: plum puddings and mincemeat pies. Today's fruity versions, made with apples and dried fruits, are just the thing to warm the heart on a blustery English day.

The comforting ritual of an abundant English tea.

M I N I A T U R E   M I N C E   P I E S

Makes 2 dozen pies

4 cups all-purpose flour	3 large eggs, lightly beaten
2⅓ cups confectioners' sugar, plus extra for dusting	¾ cup Homemade Mincemeat (recipe follows)
1 cup (2 sticks) cold unsalted butter, cut into bits	

1. In a very large bowl, stir together the flour and confectioners' sugar until they are well blended. With a pastry blender or two knives, cut in the butter until the mixture forms coarse crumbs. Gradually add the beaten eggs, tossing with a fork until the crumbs are moistened.

2. Knead the mixture gently in the bowl to form a soft dough. Divide the dough into quarters and shape each portion into a disk. Wrap each disk in plastic and refrigerate for 40 minutes, or until firm.

3. Preheat the oven to 400°F. Set out 24 patty tins, 2-inch tart pans, or individual brioche molds.

4. Roll one of the dough portions on a well-floured surface to ⅛-inch thickness. Cut out six rounds of dough with a floured 2½-inch cutter, and six rounds with a floured 2-inch cutter.

5. Making one pie at a time, fit the larger pastry rounds into the pans or molds. Spoon ½ tablespoon of the mincemeat into the center of each.

6. With a moistened finger, dampen the edges of the pastry, and place the smaller pastry rounds over the filling. Press the pastry edges together to seal. Cut a tiny hole in the top center of each pie to let the steam escape. Arrange the tart pans on baking sheets. Repeat with the remaining dough and mincemeat.

7. Bake for 12 to 15 minutes, until the pies are lightly browned. Transfer the pies to racks and let cool slightly. Remove the mincemeat pies from their pans, dust with confectioners' sugar, and serve.

PECAN SHORTBREAD COOKIES

Makes 22 cookies

Shortbread is Scottish in origin and is traditionally served at teatime. These are lovely, buttery, and not too sweet, perfect with a glass of port or eau-de-vie. Packed in a pretty box, they make a most welcome gift.

¾ cup pecans

1½ cups all-purpose flour

¼ teaspoon salt

¾ cup (1½ sticks) unsalted butter, at room temperature

½ cup confectioners' sugar

1. In a food processor, finely chop the pecans, pulsing several times. Transfer the pecans to a medium-size bowl and stir in the flour and salt.

2. Put the butter and confectioners' sugar into the processor and pulse several times, until just blended. Add the flour mixture and pulse until the dough just pulls away from the side of the bowl and forms a ball.

3. Working on a sheet of plastic wrap, pat the dough into a 6-inch square. Cover the dough with the plastic wrap and refrigerate for 30 minutes.

4. Preheat the oven to 350°F. Set out two baking sheets.

5. Roll the dough between two sheets of waxed paper into an 11-inch round, about ¼ inch thick. Peel off the top sheet of paper. Cut out cookies using a floured 2-inch cutter. Lift the rounds onto the baking sheets with a floured small metal spatula, spacing them 1 inch apart.

6. Bake for 15 minutes, or until the cookies are lightly browned. Transfer them to racks to cool completely. Store in an airtight container.

GÂTEAU DES ROIS

Makes 8 servings

Gâteau is French for "cake" and *rois* is French for "kings" ~ cake of the kings. This regal-looking yeast-leavened ring is flavored with orange flower water and topped with a citrus glaze and crushed sugar cubes. The finished cake resembles a delicious crown. Orange flower water, a clear, fragrant liquid distilled from the flowers of bitter oranges, is generally found in specialty baking or gourmet shops.

Glistening like an angel's halo, a lovely cake that's simple to make.

YEAST CAKE

1 envelope fast-rising yeast

4 large eggs, at room
  temperature

⅔ cup granulated sugar

1 tablespoon grated orange zest

1 tablespoon orange flower
  water

½ teaspoon salt

2 cups all-purpose flour

½ cup (1 stick) unsalted butter,
  well softened

ORANGE GLAZE

1 cup confectioners' sugar

1 tablespoon fresh lemon
  juice

1 teaspoon orange flower
  water

¼ cup lightly crushed sugar
  cubes

Candied fruit, for garnish

1. Butter a 9-inch springform pan that has a center tube insert.

2. To make the yeast cake, sprinkle the yeast over 2 tablespoons of warm water (105° to 110°F) in a small bowl and stir until the yeast is dissolved.

3. In the large bowl of an electric mixer, at medium-high speed, beat the eggs, granulated sugar, orange zest, orange flower water, and salt until well blended.

4. With a wooden spoon, gradually beat in the flour, butter, and yeast mixture until the batter is smooth and blended. Spoon the batter into the prepared pan, spreading it into a smooth ring shape. Place the pan on a baking sheet.

5. Cover the pan with a tea towel and let the batter rise in a warm place, away from drafts, until it is doubled in volume, about 1 hour. Preheat the oven to 400°F.

6. Bake the cake for 10 minutes. Reduce the oven temperature to 350°F and bake for 20 minutes longer, or until the cake is golden brown. Let the cake cool in the pan on a rack for 10 minutes. Then turn the cake out of the pan onto the rack to cool completely.

7. To make the orange glaze, in a small bowl, stir together the confectioners' sugar, lemon juice, and orange flower water until smooth.

8. Place a sheet of waxed paper on the counter and place the cake, still on the rack, on top of the paper. Drizzle the glaze over the cake, sprinkle it with the crushed sugar, and garnish with candied fruit.

GINGER ALMOND COOKIES

Makes 4 dozen cookies

2¼ cups all-purpose flour

1½ teaspoons baking soda

½ teaspoon salt

One 1-inch piece fresh ginger, peeled

¾ cup (1½ sticks) unsalted butter, at room temperature

1 cup packed dark brown sugar

¼ cup dark molasses

1 large egg, at room temperature

48 whole blanched almonds

1. In a medium-size bowl, stir together the flour, baking soda, and salt.

2. While a food processor is running, drop the ginger through the feed tube and process until it is finely minced.

3. Add the butter to the processor and pulse several times until it is blended. Add the brown sugar, molasses, and egg and process for 15 to 20 seconds, until the mixture is smooth.

4. Add the flour mixture all at once and pulse 2 or 3 times, just until blended. Wrap the dough in plastic and refrigerate for at least 2 or up to 8 hours, until the dough is well chilled.

5. Preheat the oven to 350°F. Lightly butter several baking sheets.

6. Roll pieces of the dough between your hands to form walnut-sized balls. Arrange the balls 2 inches apart on the prepared baking sheets. Press an almond into the center of each.

7. Bake for 14 to 16 minutes, until the cookies are firm to the touch. Transfer to racks to cool completely. Store in an airtight container.

The addition of almonds enriches one of the best-loved cookies.

A recipe close to Thomas Jefferson's, it's a lesson in simplicity.

MACAROONS

Makes 5 dozen macaroons

There are many recipes for macaroons, but the classic version is made of ground almonds, sugar, and egg whites. This is one of the baker's most versatile cookies ~ they are at home at formal and relaxed meals alike, and can be paired with fruit, ice cream, or pudding. Even the crumbs are worthy, added to crunchy toppings or sprinkled on cheesecake or fruit tarts. Unlike most macaroons, this recipe does not call for beating the egg whites into stiff peaks. Instead, these cookies get their structure from the large quantity of ground almonds.

1 pound whole blanched or
unblanched almonds

3¾ cups confectioners' sugar
(about 12 ounces)

3 large egg whites

1. To blanch the almonds (if they still have their skins), place them in a large bowl and add boiling water to cover. Drain the almonds and rub them with a tea towel to remove their skins. Put the almonds in a colander and rinse them well under cold running water. Dry the nuts thoroughly on paper towels.

2. Preheat the oven to 325°F. Line several baking sheets with parchment paper.

3. In a food processor, grind the almonds to a fine powder and then transfer them to a large bowl.

4. Gradually stir the confectioners' sugar into the almonds until well blended. Add the egg whites, one at a time, beating the mixture constantly with a wooden spoon to form a smooth paste.

5. Drop the batter in walnut-size dollops from a teaspoon onto the prepared baking sheets, spacing the dollops about 1½ inches apart.

6. Bake for 15 to 20 minutes, until the macaroons are lightly browned. Transfer them to racks to cool completely and store in an airtight container.

STRAWBERRY CHEESECAKE WITH ALMOND WHIPPED CREAM

Makes 12 servings

Here is the dessert you'll want for fine dining ~ cheesecake with strawberry sauce, almond-flavored whipped cream, and a pair of whimsical chocolate butterfly wings perched on top. The wings are fragile though, so handle them carefully.

BUTTER CRUST

Half a vanilla bean, split
    lengthwise

1 cup all-purpose flour

¼ cup sugar

1 teaspoon grated orange zest

¼ teaspoon salt

½ cup (1 stick) cold unsalted
    butter, cut into bits

1 large egg yolk

CREAM CHEESE FILLING

Five 8-ounce packages cream
    cheese, at room temperature

1¾ cups sugar

3 tablespoons all-purpose flour

1½ teaspoons grated orange zest

½ teaspoon vanilla extract

5 large eggs, at room
    temperature

2 large egg yolks, at room
    temperature

¼ cup heavy cream

1 cup thinly sliced strawberries

STRAWBERRY SAUCE

2 cups hulled strawberries

1 cup freshly squeezed orange
    juice

½ cup sugar

¼ cup orange liqueur

1 tablespoon plus 1 teaspoon
    cornstarch

CHOCOLATE WINGS

4 ounces bittersweet
    or semisweet chocolate, melt-
    ed and briefly cooled

2 ounces white chocolate, melt-
    ed and briefly cooled

ALMOND WHIPPED CREAM

1 cup heavy cream

2 tablespoons sugar

½ teaspoon vanilla extract

¼ teaspoon almond extract

Quartered strawberries,
    for garnish

1. To make the butter crust, with the tip of a small knife, scrape the seeds of the vanilla bean into a medium-size bowl. Stir in the flour, sugar, orange zest, and salt. Add the butter and the egg yolk. Knead the mixture with your fingertips until a soft dough forms. Wrap the dough in plastic and refrigerate it for 1 hour.

2. Preheat the oven to 400°F. Remove the sides of a 9-inch springform pan and lightly butter the bottom of the pan.

3. Press enough of the dough onto the pan bottom to make a layer ⅛ inch thick. Re-wrap and refrigerate the remaining dough. Place the pan on a baking sheet.

4. Bake for 10 to 12 minutes, until the crust is golden. Transfer the pan bottom to a rack and cool the crust until it is warm, then refrigerate it until it is cold.

5. Butter the sides of the springform pan and attach them to the pan bottom. Press the remaining dough three-quarters of the way up the sides of the pan, sealing it to the bottom crust.

6. Heat the oven to 500°F.

7. To make the cream cheese filling, in the large bowl of an electric mixer, at medium speed, beat the cream cheese, sugar, flour, orange zest, and vanilla until the mixture is smooth.

Parchment Cones

Precut parchment cones and triangles can be purchased in cookware stores, but it's easy to make your own. Here's how.

Cut a triangle (21 inches along its base and 15 inches from the base to the apex) from a sheet of parchment paper. Place the triangle on a work surface with the base facing you. Number the angles at the base 1 and 2 and the apex 3. To begin forming the cone, curl point 1 over and position it on point 3. While you hold points 1 and 3 with one hand, bring point 2 over and around the back of the cone so that all the points meet at point 3. Fold the three points down inside the top of the parchment cone to firmly secure it.

When the occasion is special, you have to indulge in a cheesecake.

8. Add the eggs and the egg yolks, one at a time, beating well after each addition. Beat in the cream, mixing until well blended.

9. Pour one-third of the cream cheese filling into the crust. Arrange the sliced strawberries in a layer on top of the filling. Pour the remaining filling carefully over the strawberries and place the pan on a baking sheet.

10. Bake for 12 minutes. Reduce the oven temperature to 200°F and bake for 1 to 1¼ hours longer, until the center is just firm. Let the cake cool in its pan on a rack to room temperature. Cover the cake loosely with foil and refrigerate the cake overnight.

11. On the day you plan to serve the cake, make the strawberry sauce. In a food processor, puree the strawberries, orange juice, and sugar. Press the puree through a fine-mesh strainer held over a medium-size nonreactive saucepan.

12. In a cup, stir together the orange liqueur and cornstarch until smooth.

13. Bring the strawberry puree to a boil over medium heat. Reduce the heat to medium-low and slowly pour in the cornstarch mixture, whisking constantly. Cook for 1 minute, still whisking constantly, until the sauce is thickened. Pour the sauce into a small bowl, press plastic wrap directly onto the surface, and let it cool to room temperature.

14. To make the chocolate wings, pour the dark chocolate into a parchment pastry cone and pipe the outline of 12 pairs of wings onto a waxed paper-lined baking sheet. Pour the white chocolate into another parchment cone and swirl designs inside the wings, making certain to touch the dark chocolate borders an staying within them. Refrigerate the wings for at least 10 minutes to harden, or for up to 3 days.

15. Just before serving, make the almond whipped cream. In the chilled medium-size bowl of the mixer, at high speed, beat the cream until soft peaks form. Add the sugar, vanilla, and almond extract and beat until stiff peaks form.

16. To serve, cut the cheesecake into 12 wedges with a knife that has been dipped into hot water. Spoon the strawberry sauce onto dessert plates and place a wedge of cheesecake on top of the sauce. Garnish each serving with a spoonful of the almond whipped cream, a pair of the chocolate wings, and quartered strawberries. Refrigerate any leftovers.

BURNT SUGAR CREAM CAKE

Makes 12 servings

CREAM CAKE

2 cups all-purpose flour

1¼ cups sugar

1 tablespoon baking powder

¾ teaspoon salt

1¼ cups heavy cream

3 large eggs, at room
   temperature

1½ teaspoons vanilla extract

1 recipe Burnt Sugar Syrup (page
   82)

18 fresh or drained, canned
   peach slices

18 fresh or drained, canned
   pear slices

CREAM TOPPING

1 cup heavy cream

Burnt Sugar Crunch
   (page 196), for garnish

1. Preheat the oven to 350°F. Generously butter a 12-cup fluted tube pan. Dust the pan with flour, shaking out the excess.

2. To make the cream cake, sift together the flour, sugar, baking powder, and salt.

3. In the chilled large bowl of an electric mixer, at high speed, beat the cream until it holds its shape, and then refrigerate the cream.

4. Wash the beaters. Crack the eggs into the small bowl of the mixer, and add the vanilla. Beat at high speed until the eggs are thick and lemon-colored, about 6 minutes. With a rubber spatula, fold the beaten eggs into the whipped cream.

5. Gradually drizzle ¼ cup of the burnt sugar syrup over the egg mixture, gently folding in each addition. Gradually sift in the flour and fold it in until it is well blended. Gently and evenly spread the batter in the prepared pan.

6. Bake for 45 minutes, or until the cake pulls away from the side of the pan and a toothpick inserted in the center comes out clean. (The cake will not fill the pan.)

7. Let the cake cool in the pan on a rack for about 10 minutes. Then run a thin metal spatula around the edge of the pan to loosen the cake and turn it out of the pan onto the rack.

Complex and daring, a dramatic cake takes time. But oh, those sighs!

8. Set the rack over a jelly-roll pan and use a skewer to poke holes all over the top and sides of the cake. Brush the cake with 2 to 3 tablespoons of the burnt sugar syrup. As the cake cools, continue brushing it with more syrup, a few tablespoons at a time. Let the cake cool completely.

9. Meanwhile, blot the peach and pear slices dry on sheets of paper towel. Place the fruit on a plate and brush it lightly with a little of the burnt sugar syrup, using just enough of the syrup to glaze the fruit.

10. Just before you are ready to serve, make the cream topping. In the chilled small bowl of the mixer, at high speed, beat the cream until soft peaks form. Add 2 tablespoons of the burnt sugar syrup, beating until stiff peaks form.

11. Place the cake on a serving plate and decorate it with the peach and pear slices. Spoon the cream topping into the center of the cake and sprinkle the cream with the burnt sugar crunch. Refrigerate any leftovers.

A taste of the Highlands weaves through this elegant soufflé.

DRAMBUIE CUSTARD SOUFFLÉ

Makes 6 servings

Drambuie is a liqueur from Scotland, a marriage of scotch whisky and heather honey. For this dish, you can substitute amaretto or Cointreau, if you wish. Bake the soufflé in gold-colored dishes for the most dramatic presentation.

DRAMBUIE ANGLAISE

2 cups heavy cream

½ cup granulated sugar

1 vanilla bean, split lengthwise

5 large egg yolks

2 tablespoons Drambuie

SOUFFLÉ

1⅓ cups milk

¼ cup granulated sugar, plus extra for the dishes

Half a vanilla bean, split lengthwise

4 tablespoons unsalted butter

½ cup plus 1½ tablespoons all-purpose flour

5 large egg yolks

¼ cup honey (preferably orange blossom)

¼ cup Drambuie

7 large egg whites, at room temperature

Confectioners' sugar, for garnish

Honeycomb, for garnish (optional)

1. To make the Drambuie anglaise, in a heavy medium-size saucepan, bring the cream, sugar, and one half of the vanilla bean to a boil over medium heat, stirring to dissolve the sugar. Remove from the heat.

2. In the top of a double boiler, whisk the egg yolks until they are pale and thick. Gradually whisk in the hot cream. Place the double boiler over simmering water and cook, stirring constantly with a wooden spoon, until the mixture thickens slightly and an instant-read or candy thermometer registers 175°F.

3. Pour the sauce into a medium-size bowl. Press plastic wrap directly onto the

surface and refrigerate until it is just cool. Remove the vanilla bean and stir in the Drambuie. Again, press plastic wrap directly onto the surface and refrigerate for at least 4 hours, or for up to 2 days.

4. Next, make the soufflé. In a small heavy saucepan, bring the milk, sugar, and the remaining vanilla bean half to a boil over medium heat, stirring to dissolve the sugar. Remove from the heat. At the same time, in another small saucepan, bring the butter to a boil over medium heat. Watch the butter closely, to make sure it doesn't scorch. Remove the butter from the heat.

5. In the large bowl of an electric mixer, at medium speed, beat together the flour and boiling butter until a smooth paste forms.

6. Remove the vanilla bean from the milk. Slowly pour the milk into the butter mixture, beating until a sticky batter forms. Continue beating the batter until it has cooled until just warm to the touch, about 8 minutes.

7. Add the egg yolks, one at a time, beating until fully blended after each addition. Let the mixture cool for 10 minutes, then beat in the honey and Drambuie. Scrape the batter into a large bowl and wash the mixer bowl and beaters.

8. Preheat the oven to 325°F and butter six 10- to 12-ounce individual soufflé dishes. Dust the dishes with granulated sugar, turning to coat the sides, and shake out the excess sugar.

9. In the large bowl of the mixer, at high speed, beat the egg whites until stiff peaks form when the beaters are lifted. With a large rubber spatula, fold the beaten whites into the Drambuie batter.

10. Spoon about 1 cup of the batter into each prepared soufflé dish. Arrange the dishes in a large shallow baking pan. Pour hot water around the dishes to reach a depth of one inch.

11. Bake the soufflés for 30 to 35 minutes, until they are puffed and a toothpick inserted in the center comes out clean.

12. To serve, gently make a break in the top of each soufflé with two forks placed back to back. Spoon a little of the Drambuie anglaise into each soufflé and then sift confectioners' sugar over the tops. If desired, garnish the souffles with small pieces of honeycomb, and serve them right away.

HARVEST MOON CAKE

Makes 8 to 10 servings

GENOISE

1 cup all-purpose flour

½ cup finely ground almonds

6 large eggs, separated

1 cup granulated sugar

3 tablespoons unsalted butter, melted and cooled

FROSTING

¾ cup (1½ sticks) unsalted butter, at room temperature

3 cups confectioners' sugar

¼ cup Triple Sec or another orange liqueur

WHITE CHOCOLATE MOUSSE

8 ounces white chocolate, coarsely chopped

1½ cups heavy cream

½ cup apricot preserves, warmed and strained

½ cup melted and cooled cranberry or red currant jelly, for spreading

Pomegranates, cranberries, dried apricots and almonds, for garnish

1. Preheat the oven to 350°F. Butter two 8- by 1½-inch layer-cake pans. Dust the pans with flour, shaking out the excess.

2. To make the genoise, sift the flour and almonds through a fine-mesh strainer.

3. In the medium-size bowl of an electric mixer, at high speed, beat the egg yolks and ¾ cup of the granulated sugar until the eggs are thick and lemon-colored, about 6 minutes. Reduce the mixer speed to medium and gradually beat in the melted butter.

4. Wash the beaters. In the large bowl of the mixer, at high speed, beat the egg whites until they are foamy. Gradually add the remaining ¼ cup of granulated sugar, beating until almost stiff peaks form.

5. With a large rubber spatula, fold the yolk mixture into the whites, one-third at a time. Sift one-third of the flour mixture over the top and fold it in until no dry pockets of flour remain. Repeat the sifting and folding process twice more.

6. Pour the batter into the prepared pans, tilting the pans to gently and carefully

spread the batter to the edges of the baking pans, smoothing the batter evenly.

7. Bake for 20 to 30 minutes, until the cakes are light golden brown, slightly shrink from the side of the pans, and they spring back when they are gently touched in the center.

8. Let the cakes cool in the pans on racks for 10 minutes. Run a metal spatula around the edge of the pans to loosen the cakes and turn them out onto the racks to cool completely.

9. To make the frosting, in the large bowl of the mixer, at medium-high speed, beat the butter until it is light and creamy. Gradually beat in the confectioners' sugar until the mixture is smooth and fluffy, scraping the side of the bowl often. Beat in the Triple Sec. Cover the frosting with plastic wrap and set aside.

10. Next make the white chocolate mousse. In the top of a double boiler, over barely simmering water, melt the white chocolate and ¼ cup of the cream, stirring frequently, until smooth. Remove from the heat and cool the mixture for about 20 minutes, or until it is warm, stirring often.

11. In the chilled medium-size bowl of the mixer, at high speed, beat the remaining 1¼ cups of cream until stiff peaks form.

12. Quickly stir ½ cup of the whipped cream into the cooled chocolate mixture. Then quickly fold the chocolate mixture into the remaining whipped cream until it is completely blended. Fold in the apricot preserves.

13. With a large serrated knife, cut each cake in half horizontally. Arrange one cake layer on a serving plate and spread it with one-third of the mousse. Stack two more cake layers on top of the first, spreading each cake layer with one-third of the mousse. Top with the remaining layer, placing it cut side down.

14. Set aside ½ cup of the frosting. Frost the cake top and sides with the remaining frosting. Cover the cake loosely and refrigerate for 1½ hours, or until it is set.

15. Fit a small pastry bag with a small star tip and fill it with the reserved frosting. Pipe a decorative border along the top edge of the cake. Spoon the cooled cranberry jelly over the top of the cake, gently spreading it within the piped border. Refrigerate for at least 3 hours, or until you are ready to serve.

16. Garnish the cake with the fruit and almonds. Refrigerate any leftovers.

Pomegranates have featured in the cuisines of the Middle East and parts of the Mediterranean for thousands of years. Throughout history they have been a symbol of fertility and prosperity; and even have their own footnote in Greek mythology.

This exotic fruit is only picked when it is already fully ripe. When you buy them, choose those that feel heavy and are unblemished. Use a sharp knife to cut through the thick skin, and then separate the juicy seeds from the cream-colored membrane (which you can discard, along with the skin). Pomegranates will keep for several days at room temperature, or in the refrigerator for up to several weeks.

PANTRY

SUGAR SYRUP

Makes ½ cup

¼ cup sugar

1. In a small heavy saucepan, stir together the sugar with ¼ cup of cold water. Cook over medium heat, stirring frequently to dissolve the sugar, until the syrup comes to a boil.

2. Remove from the heat and let the syrup cool to room temperature. Store in a covered jar in the refrigerator for up to three months.

VANILLA SUGAR

Makes 3½ to 4 cups

1 vanilla bean

One 1-pound box confectioners' sugar or 4 cups granulated sugar

1. Bury the vanilla bean in the center of the box of confectioners' sugar, or in an airtight container of the granulated sugar.

2. Cover the sugar and let it stand at room temperature for 4 to 7 days, or until the sugar has absorbed the scent of the vanilla.

CRÈME ANGLAISE

Makes 2 cups

3 large egg yolks

¼ cup sugar

2 cups half-and-half

2 tablespoons Grand Marnier

1 vanilla bean, split lengthwise

1. In the large bowl of an electric mixer, at high speed, beat the egg yolks and sugar until thick and lemon-colored, about 6 minutes.
2. In a medium-size heavy saucepan, bring the half-and-half, Grand Marnier, and vanilla bean just to boiling over medium heat. Remove the pan from the heat and discard the vanilla bean.
3. With the mixer on low speed, very slowly beat the hot cream into the egg yolks. Return the mixture to a clean heavy saucepan.
4. Cook over medium-low heat, stirring constantly with a wooden spoon, until the custard coats the back of the spoon.
5. Immediately pour the sauce into a medium-size bowl and set the bowl in a larger bowl of ice water. Cool, stirring occasionally. Press plastic wrap directly onto the surface of the sauce and refrigerate until you are ready to serve. Refrigerate the sauce for up to three days.

RASPBERRY SAUCE

Makes 1 cup

One 10-ounce package frozen raspberries in syrup, thawed, with its juice

2 tablespoons raspberry jam

2 tablespoons raspberry liqueur

1. In a food processor, puree the raspberries and their juice along with the jam. Press the puree through a fine-mesh strainer set over a small bowl. Stir the raspberry liqueur into the puree.
2. Cover and chill the raspberry puree until you are ready to serve.

KIWI SAUCE

Makes 1 cup

6 kiwis, peeled and quartered

¼ cup light corn syrup

2 tablespoons melon liqueur

1 tablespoon unflavored gelatin

1. In a food processor, puree the kiwi until smooth.
2. Stir in the corn syrup and liqueur.
3. Pour the puree into a small saucepan, sprinkle the gelatin over, and let stand for 5 minutes. Simmer the puree, stirring, over low heat, until the gelatin is dissolved.
4. Transfer the kiwi sauce to a small bowl. Cover and refrigerate until ready to use.

HARD SAUCE

Makes 1 cup

1 cup (2 sticks) unsalted butter, at
  room temperature

1¼ cups confectioners' sugar, sifted

3 to 4 tablespoons brandy

2 teaspoons grated orange zest
  (optional)

1 tablespoon freshly squeezed
  orange juice

1. In the medium-size bowl of an electric mixer, at
high speed, beat the butter and sugar until light
and fluffy, scraping down the sides of the bowl.

2. Reduce the mixer speed to medium and gradually beat in the brandy. Beat in the orange zest if
using, and the orange juice. Transfer the hard
sauce to a small serving bowl.

3. If you are serving the sauce within a few hours,
leave it at room temperature. Otherwise, cover
and refrigerate the sauce, but let it come to room
temperature before serving.

BURNT SUGAR
SYRUP

Makes 1 cup plus 2 tablespoons

1 cup sugar

1 cup boiling water

1. Place the sugar in a large heavy saucepan over

medium-high heat. Cook, stirring occasionally,
until the sugar melts and the syrup turns dark
amber.

2. Reduce the heat to medium-low. Using a long-
handled spoon, and protecting your hands with
oven mitts, add the boiling water, 1 tablespoon
at a time, stirring vigorously. Be careful—the
mixture will boil up and spatter, especially at
first. If necessary, after adding all the water, continue cooking and stirring the syrup to dissolve
any lumps of caramel that have formed.

3. Cool the syrup thoroughly before using it in
recipes. The cooled syrup can be stored in a covered jar in the refrigerator for up to a month.

BURNT SUGAR
CRUNCH

Makes about 1 cup

1 cup sugar

Softened unsalted butter

1. Preheat the broiler. Line a heavy baking sheet
with a double thickness of heavy-duty foil.

2. Pour the sugar onto the center of the foil and
spread the sugar into a ¼-inch thick layer leaving
a 2-inch foil border. (The rectangle should measure approximately 12- by 7- inches.) Generously
butter the foil border. It will help keep the sugar
in place as it melts.

3. Broil the sugar 4 to 5 inches from the heat, until

the sugar melts and turns a deep caramel color. Watch carefully to see that the sugar doesn't burn.

4. Place the baking sheet on a rack and let it cool completely. Remove the sugar from the foil and break it into large pieces. To crush the sugar, place the pieces in a heavy-gauge plastic bag and pound it with a meat pounder or rolling pin. Transfer the burnt sugar crunch to an airtight container and store at room temperature for up to two months.

CHOCOLATE LEAVES

Makes 10 to 12 chocolate leaves

10 to 12 fresh firm pesticide-free green leaves, preferably gardenia, ivy, rose, lemon, or other non-toxic firm leaves

2 ounces semisweet chocolate, coarsely chopped

1. Wash and thoroughly dry the leaves.

2. Melt the chocolate in the top of a double boiler over barely simmering water. Stir until the chocolate is smooth. Remove from the heat.

3. With a table knife, spread a thin, even layer of chocolate on the back of each leaf, being careful to spread to, but not over, the edge of each leaf. The leaf should be completely coated with chocolate.

4. Place the leaves, chocolate side up, on a baking sheet. Set in a cool, dry place until the

chocolate is firm. (Refrigerating will set the chocolate in a few minutes, but it may also cause a white bloom to form.)

5. To use the chocolate leaves, just before serving, remove each chocolate leaf from each green leaf by gently pulling the green leaf by the stem, up and away from the chocolate.

6. Arrange the chocolate leaves decoratively on top of a cake, pie, or other dessert and serve.

SUGARED GRAPES OR MINT LEAVES

Makes 6 grape clusters or 30 mint leaves

6 small grape clusters or 30 mint leaves

1 egg white, lightly beaten or 4 ounces frozen egg substitute, thawed

Sugar

1. One at a time, dip the grape clusters or mint leaves in the egg white.

2. Roll the grapes, or press the mint leaves on both sides, in the sugar. Arrange in a single layer on sheets of parchment paper and let them dry for at least 12 hours.

3. Store, layered with waxed paper, in an airtight container in the refrigerator.

CRYSTALLIZED PETALS AND FLOWERS

Makes several dozen

1 egg white or 4 ounces frozen egg substitute, thawed

Pesticide-free edible flowers, such as borage, lavender, marigolds, calendula, roses, rose petals, violets, primrose, or daisy blossoms

Superfine sugar

1. In a small bowl, beat the egg white with a whisk until frothy. With a small brush, lightly paint the flowers and petals on all sides with the egg white. Heavily dust the flowers and petals with superfine sugar. Put the flowers on a rack at room temperature and set them aside until they are dry and crisp.

2. Store, layered with waxed paper, in an airtight container in the refrigerator.

RICH AND TENDER DOUGH

Makes one 9-inch double-crust pie or two 9-inch pastry shells

1 large egg yolk

1½ teaspoons cider vinegar

2 cups all-purpose flour

2 teaspoons sugar

1 teaspoon salt

¾ cup plus 2 tablespoons chilled solid white vegetable shortening, cut into bits

1. In a small bowl, whisk together ¼ cup of ice water, the egg yolk, and vinegar until blended.

2. In a large bowl, whisk together the flour, sugar, and salt. With a pastry blender, cut in the shortening until the mixture forms a coarse meal.

3. Gradually add the egg mixture, stirring with a fork, until it is all moistened and the dough begins to pull away from the side of the bowl. Gather the dough into a ball.

4. Divide the dough in half and shape each piece into a disk. Wrap the dough in plastic and refrigerate for at least 30 minutes, or overnight.

CHARLOTTE'S PIE CRUST

Makes one 9- or 10-inch double-crust pie or

two 9-inch pastry shells

2 cups all-purpose flour

½ teaspoon baking powder

½ teaspoon salt

½ cup (1 stick) cold unsalted butter, cut into bits

½ cup solid white vegetable shortening, cut into bits

1 large egg

1 tablespoon cider vinegar

1. In a large bowl, stir together the flour, baking powder, and salt. With a pastry blender or two knives, cut in the butter and shortening until the mixture forms a coarse meal.

2. In a small bowl, whisk ¼ cup plus 1 tablespoon of ice water, the egg, and vinegar until blended.

3. Gradually pour the egg mixture into the flour mixture, stirring with a fork until the dough is moistened. Gather the dough into a ball.

4. Divide the dough into two-third and one-third portions for a double-crust pie, or in half for two pastry shells. Shape each piece into a disk, wrap the dough in plastic, and refrigerate for at least 1 hour, or until chilled.

OLD-FASHIONED DOUGH

Makes one 9- or 10-inch double-crust pie or

two 9-inch pastry shells

2½ cups all-purpose flour

1 tablespoon sugar

1 teaspoon salt

½ cup (1 stick) cold unsalted butter, cut into bits

½ cup chilled solid white vegetable shortening, cut into 1-inch chunks

1 large egg

1. In a large bowl, stir together the flour, sugar, and salt. With a pastry blender or two knives, cut in the butter and shortening until the mixture forms a coarse meal.

2. In a small bowl, whisk together the egg and ¼ cup of ice water. Gradually pour the egg mixture into the flour mixture, stirring with a fork, until the dough begins to cling together but before it forms a ball.

3. Turn the dough out onto a lightly floured work surface. Lightly work the dough with the heel of your hand or your fingertips until the dough begins to form a ball.

4. Divide the dough into two-third and one-third portions for a double-crust pie, or in half for two pastry shells. Shape each piece into a disk, wrap the dough in plastic, and refrigerate for at least 2 hours, or overnight.

SWEET BISCUIT DOUGH

Makes six 3-inch biscuits or fourteen
2-inch biscuits.

1¾ cups all-purpose flour

2 tablespoons sugar

2 teaspoons baking powder

½ teaspoon baking soda

¼ teaspoon freshly grated nutmeg
  or ground cinnamon

¼ teaspoon salt

3 tablespoons solid white vegetable
  shortening

2 tablespoons cold unsalted butter,
  cut into bits

¾ cup buttermilk

1. In a large bowl, stir together the flour, the sugar, baking powder, baking soda, nutmeg, and salt. With a pastry blender or two knives, cut in the shortening and butter until the mixture forms a coarse meal.

2. Stir in the buttermilk until a soft dough forms. Turn the dough out onto a well-floured surface and knead it gently with your fingertips about 10 times, or until smooth. Do not overwork the dough or the biscuits will be tough.

3. Proceed according to recipe.

HOMEMADE MINCEMEAT

1⅓ cups dark raisins

1⅓ cups golden raisins

⅔ cup chopped candied orange and
  lemon peel

1 pound tart apples, peeled, cored and
  chopped
  (2½ cups)

3 cups currants

2¼ cups packed light or dark brown
  sugar

Grated zest and juice of 2
  medium-size lemons

1 teaspoon pumpkin-pie spice

1. Chop the raisins and candied peel in a food processor or by hand. Put into a large bowl and add the apples, currants, brown sugar, lemon zest and juice, pumpkin-pie spice, ginger, and nutmeg, stirring to mix well. Cover tightly with plastic wrap and let stand overnight.

2. Stir in the brandy. Pack the mincemeat into sterilized jars, cover, and refrigerate for up to six weeks. Stir well before using.

INDEX

RECIPE CREDITS

A. J. BATAFARANO
Vanilla Confectioner's Sugar
Vanilla Hazelnut Biscotti

PHILIS BENNETT
Apple Cake
Burnt Sugar Cookies
Burnt Sugar Cream Cake
Burnt Sugar Crunch
Burnt Sugar Syrup

CHARLOTTE BERO
Charlotte's Pie Crust
Cherry-Filled Scones
Cherry Nutbread
Lemon Squares
Sour Cherry Pie
Strawberry Rhubarb Custard Pie

MICHELLE BERRIEDALE-
JOHNSON
Bakewell Tart

TERESE BLANDING
Tearoom Peaches

GLORIA BOEHNER
Brownie Torte

BOOKBINDER'S
Old Original Bookbinder's
    Apple Walnut Pie

FRANK BROUGH
Drambuie Custard Soufflé

CAFE LOUIS
Flourless Chocolate Cake

CAFE MOZART
Strawberry Cheesecake with
    Almond Whipped Cream

CAFE VICTORIA
Cafe Victoria's Apple Dumplings

CEDAR GROVE
PLANTATION
Kiwi Sauce
Raspberry Sauce

MOLLY CHAPPELLET
Orange Whipped Cream Cake

JOHN CLANCY
John Clancy's Pound Cake

DEMEL'S
Truffle Cake

TERESA
DOUGLAS-MITCHELL
Champagne Chestnut Torte

BETTY JEAN DYVIG
Tea and Button Tarts

DOMINIQUE
FERSZTENFELD
Apricot Prune Tartlets
Gateau des Rois

JOHN FLEER
Rum Pecan Pie

JEAN-PAUL and MARIE
MAGDELEINE GRUHIER
Plum Tart

HELEN GUSTAFSON
Ginger Lemon Hearts

MARY HARMON
Whidbey Island Loganberry
    Liqueur Cake

AUDREY and VIVIAN
HEREDIA
Meringue Basket with Berries
Peaches and Cream Cake

ROSEMARY HOWE
Victoria Sponge

SUE HURD MACHAMEK
Pear Meringue Tart

THOMAS JEFFERSON
Gingerbread
Macaroons

KERI KAZEL
Strawberry Cream Pie with
   Almond Pastry
Strawberry Shortcake

LA FLUTE GANA
Apple Clafoutis

LITTLE PIE COMPANY
Lemon Meringue Pie
Old-Fashioned Dough
Rich Tender Dough

LILLY McNAUGHT
Tea Cakes with Marmalade

SUSAN MANOLIS
Pumpkin Tart with Cranberry Fool

THE MANOR
Sugared Grapes

MICHAEL'S NOOK
Hard Sauce

NETHERFIELD PLACE
Pastry Gateaux with Raspberry
   and Cream

OLD RITTENHOUSE
White Chocolate Muffins

MARLENE PARRISH
Ginger Almond Cookies

PAT REPPERT
Lemon Thyme Poppies

RESTAURANT MARCH
March's Warm Chocolate Cake

RIVER WILDLIFE
Dutch Apple Tart

MEG RIVERS
Almond Fruitcake

ROYAL CRESCENT
HOTEL
Coconut Shortbread
Christmas Cake
Homemade Mincemeat
Miniature Mince Pies
Royal Crescent Scones

RUSSIAN TEA ROOM
Sacher Torte
Sugar Syrup

SAGAMORE INSTITUTE
Cardamom Coffee Breads

BRENDA SMELTZ
Harvest Moon Cake

SORREL HOUSE
Brandied Pumpkin Pie

EMILIE TOLLEY
Orange Poppy Seed Cake

WINDSOR COURT
HOTEL
Dundee Cake

PHOTOGRAPHY
CREDITS

Page

2: Toshi Otsuki

4: Steve Randazzo

6: (top) Toshi Otsuki
(bottom) Bryan E. McCay

7: (top) William P. Steele
(middle) Pierre Chanteau
(bottom) Katrina

8: Kari Haavisto

10: William P. Steele

11: Tina Mucci

13: William P. Steele

15: Joshua Greene

16: Tina Mucci

17: Nicolas Millet

19: Michael Skott

23: Tom Eckerle

27: Toshi Otsuki

29: Katrina

31: William P. Steele

33: Katrina

35: Pierre Hussenot

36: Pierre Chanteau (both)

39: William P. Steele

41: William P. Steele

42: Michael Skott

43: Alan Weintraub

47: William P. Steele

49: Toshi Otsuki

50: Pierre Chanteau

55: William P. Steele

56: Guy Bouchet

57: Guy Bouchet

59: William P. Steele

63: Rosemary Weller

64: Toshi Otsuki

65: Tom Eckerle

69: Steve Cohen

72: Toshi Otsuki

74: Toshi Otsuki

75: Toshi Otsuki

79: Pierre Chanteau

81: William P. Steele

83: John Kane

84: Pierre Chanteau

88: William P. Steele

90: Toshi Otsuki

91: Bill Tyler

93: Toshi Otsuki

96: Hedrich Blessing

99: William P. Steele

101: Michael Skott

102: William P. Steele

105: William P. Steele

107: William P. Steele

109: William P. Steele

110: William P. Steele

111: William P. Steele

113: Jeremy Samuelson

115: William P. Steele

117: Pierre Chanteau

118: Kit Latham

120: Doreen Wynja

122: William P. Steele

123: William P. Steele

125: Katrina

127: William P. Steele

129: Pierre Hussenot

131: Toshi Otsuki

135: Tom Eckerle

137: William P. Steele

144: Katrina

145: Robert Brenner, Lissa
Bryan-Smith, Rinker Enterprises

147: Bryan E. McCay

149: Jim Hedrich

150: Steve Cohen

154: Pierre Hussenot

155: Pierre Hussenot

157: Toshi Otsuki

159: Michael Skott

160: William P. Steele

163: William P. Steele

165: Hedrich Blessing

167: Pierre Chanteau

169: Toshi Otsuki

170: Toshi Otsuki

171: Toshi Otsuki

174: Nicolas Millet

177: Joshua Greene

178: Jim Hedrich

182: William P. Steele

185: John Kane

186: Tom Eckerle

191: Toshi Otsuki

193: Pierre Hussenot